MW01174746

Illustrative IFRS consolidated
financial statements for 2013 year ends

Global Accounting Consulting Services
PricewaterhouseCoopers LLP

Published by

Bloomsbury Professional

Bloomsbury Professional, an imprint of Bloomsbury Publishing Plc, Maxwelton House, 41–43 Boltro Road, Haywards Heath, West Sussex, RH16 1BJ

ISBN 9781780432588

British Library Cataloguing-in-Publication Data.
A catalogue record for this book is available from the British Library.

© 2013 PricewaterhouseCoopers

Printed in Great Britain

IFRS GAAP plc – year ended 31 December 2013

Introduction

This publication provides an illustrative set of consolidated financial statements, prepared in accordance with International Financial Reporting Standards (IFRS), for a fictional manufacturing, wholesale and retail group (IFRS GAAP plc).

IFRS GAAP plc is an existing preparer of IFRS consolidated financial statements; IFRS 1, 'First-time adoption of International Financial Reporting Standards', is not applicable. Guidance on financial statements for first-time adopters of IFRS is available at www.pwc.com/ifrs

This publication is based on the requirements of IFRS standards and interpretations for financial years beginning on or after 1 January 2013.

PwC commentary has been provided, in grey boxes, to explain the detail behind the presentation of a number of challenging areas. We draw your attention in particular to our commentary on the income statement, statement of comprehensive income, balance sheet, statement of changes in equity, statement of cash flows, statement of significant accounting policies and financial risk management.

> Areas in which we have made significant changes to presentation since 2012 have been highlighted in pink. For 2013 the significant changes include the application of IFRSs 10, 11, 12 and 13 together with IAS 19 and the IAS 1 presentation changes to Other Comprehensive Income.

We have attempted to create a realistic set of financial statements for a corporate entity. However, by necessity we illustrate disclosures that for many entities may be immaterial. Determining the level of disclosure is a matter of judgement, and naturally disclosure of immaterial items is not required. Certain types of transaction have been excluded, as they are not relevant to the group's operations. The example disclosures, if material, for some of these additional items have been included in appendix III. The forthcoming IFRS requirements are outlined in a table in appendix IV.

The example disclosures should not be considered the only acceptable form of presentation. The form and content of each reporting entity's financial statements are the responsibility of the entity's management. Alternative presentations to those proposed in this publication may be equally acceptable if they comply with the specific disclosure requirements prescribed in IFRS.

These illustrative financial statements are not a substitute for reading the standards and interpretations themselves or for professional judgement as to fairness of presentation. They do not cover all possible disclosures that IFRS requires. Further specific information may be required in order to ensure fair presentation under IFRS. We recommend that readers refer to our publication *IFRS disclosure checklist 2013*.

Abbreviations

IFRS1p37 = International Financial Reporting Standard [number], paragraph number.

7p22 = International Accounting Standard [number], paragraph number.

SIC-15p5 = Standing Interpretations Committee [number], paragraph number.

DV = Disclosure Voluntary. Disclosure is encouraged but not required and therefore represents best practice.

Contents

Contents

(All amounts in C thousands unless otherwise stated)

Consolidated income statement[1]

1p10(b)

		Note	Year ended 31 December	
1p113, 1p38			2013	2012 Restated
	Continuing operations			
1p82(a)	Revenue	5	**211,034**	112,360
1p99, 1p103	Cost of sales	6	**(77,366)**	(46,682)
1p103	**Gross profit[2]**		**133,668**	65,678
1p99, 1p103	Distribution costs		**(52,529)**	(21,213)
1p99, 1p103	Administrative expenses		**(30,105)**	(10,511)
1p99, 1p103	Other income	7	**2,750**	1,259
1p85	Other (losses)/gains – net	8	**(90)**	63
1p85	**Operating profit[2]**		**53,694**	35,276
1p85	Finance income	11	**1,730**	1,609
1p82(b)	Finance costs	11	**(8,173)**	(12,197)
1p85	Finance costs – net	11	**(6,443)**	(10,588)
1p82(c)	Share of profit of investments accounted for using the equity method	12	**1,682**	1,022
1p85	**Profit before income tax**		**48,933**	25,710
1p82(d),12p77	Income tax expense	13	**(14,611)**	(8,670)
1p85	**Profit for the year from continuing operations**		**34,322**	17,040
IFRS5p33(a)	**Discontinued operations**			
	Profit for the year from discontinued operations (attributable to owners of the parent)	25	**100**	120
1p81A(a)	**Profit for the year**		**34,422**	17,160
	Profit attributable to:			
1p81B(a)(ii)	– Owners of the parent		**31,874**	16,304
1p81B(a)(i), IFRS12p12(e)	– Non-controlling interests	12	**2,548**	856
			34,422	17,160
	Earnings per share from continuing and discontinued operations attributable to owners of the parent during the year (expressed in C per share)			
	Basic earnings per share			
33p66	From continuing operations	14	**1.35**	0.79
33p68	From discontinued operations[3]		**0.01**	0.01
33p66	From profit for the year		**1.36**	0.80
	Diluted earnings per share			
33p66	From continuing operations	14	**1.21**	0.74
33p68	From discontinued operations		**0.01**	0.01
33p66	From profit for the year		**1.22**	0.75

The notes on pages 22 to 150 are an integral part of these consolidated financial statements.

[1] This income statement presents expenses by function. See Commentary, paras 12 and 13.
[2] IAS 1 does not prescribe the disclosure of operating profit and gross profit on the face of the income statement. However, entities are not prohibited from disclosing this or a similar line item.
[3] EPS for discontinued operations may be given in the notes to the financial statements instead of the income statement.

(All amounts in C thousands unless otherwise stated)

Consolidated statement of comprehensive income

		Note	2013	2012 Restated
			Year ended 31 December	
	Profit for the year		**34,422**	17,160
	Other comprehensive income:			
1p82A	**Items that will not be reclassified to profit or loss**			
16p39	Gains on revaluation of land and buildings	29	755	759
19p93B	Remeasurements of post employment benefit obligations	28,33	83	(637)
			838	122
1p82A	**Items that may be subsequently reclassified to profit or loss**			
IFRS7p20(a)(ii)	Change in value of available-for-sale financial assets	29	362	912
IFRS3p59	Reclassification of revaluation of previously held interest in ABC Group	7,29,39	(850)	–
1p85	Impact of change in Euravian tax rate on deferred tax[1]	28,32	(10)	–
IFRS7p23(c)	Cash flow hedges	29	64	(3)
1p85	Net investment hedge	29	(45)	40
21p52(b)	Currency translation differences	29	2,401	(922)
1p82A	Share of other comprehensive income of investments accounted for using the equity method	29	(86)	91
			1,836	118
	Other comprehensive income for the year, net of tax	13	2,674	240
1p81A(c)	**Total comprehensive income for the year**		**37,096**	17,400
	Attributable to:			
1p81B(b)(ii)	– Owners of the parent		34,296	16,584
1p81B(b)(i)	– Non-controlling interests	12	2,800	816
	Total comprehensive income for the year		**37,096**	17,400
	Total comprehensive income attributable to equity shareholders arises from:			
	– Continuing operations		34,196	16,464
IFRS5p33(d)	– Discontinued operations	25	100	120
			34,296	16,584

Items in the statement above are disclosed net of tax. The income tax relating to each component of other comprehensive income is disclosed in note 13.

The notes on pages 22 to 150 are an integral part of these consolidated financial statements.

[1] The impact of change in Euravian tax rate is shown for illustrative purposes.

(All amounts in C thousands unless otherwise stated)

Commentary — income statement and statement of comprehensive income

The commentary that follows explains some of the key requirements in IAS 1, 'Presentation of financial statements', and other requirements that impact the income statement/statement of comprehensive income.

1p10A

1. Entities have a choice of presenting a statement of profit and loss and other comprehensive income:
   (a) An entity may present a single statement of profit or loss and other comprehensive income, with profit or loss and other comprehensive income presented in two sections. The sections shall be presented together, with the profit or loss section presented first followed directly by the other comprehensive income section; or
   (b) An entity may present the profit or loss section in a separate statement of profit or loss. If so, the separate statement of profit or loss shall immediately precede the statement presenting comprehensive income, which shall begin with profit or loss.

The main difference between these two options is that in option (a), profit for the year is shown as a sub-total rather than the 'bottom line', and the statement continues down to total comprehensive income for the year.

1p81A

2. The statement of profit and loss and other comprehensive income shall include:
   (a) profit or loss
   (b) total other comprehensive income
   (c) comprehensive income for the period, being the total of (a) and (b)

1p81B

3. The following items are disclosed as allocations for the period:
   (a) profit or loss attributable to:
      (i) non-controlling interests; and
      (ii) owners of the parent
   (b) total comprehensive income for the period attributable to:
      (i) non-controlling interests; and
      (ii) owners of the parent

IFRS5p33(d)
   (c) the amount of income attributable to owners of the parent from:
      (i) continuing operations; and
      (ii) discontinued operations.

1p82

4. The profit or loss section or the statement of profit and loss includes, as a minimum, the following line items:
   (a) revenue;
   (b) finance costs;
   (c) share of the profit or loss of associates and joint ventures accounted for using the equity method;
   (d) tax expense;
   (e) a single amount for the total of discontinued operations.

1p82A

5. The other comprehensive income section shall present items classified by nature (including share of the other comprehensive income of associates and joint ventures accounted for using the equity method) and grouped in those that, in accordance with other IFRSs:
   (a) will not be reclassified subsequently to profit or loss; and

(All amounts in C thousands unless otherwise stated)

(b) will be reclassified subsequently to profit or loss when specific conditions are met.

1p85   6. Additional line items, headings and subtotals are presented in the statement of comprehensive income and the income statement (where presented) when such presentation is relevant to an understanding of the entity's financial performance.

7. Additional sub-headings should be used with care. The apparent flexibility in IAS 1 can only be used to enhance users' understanding of the GAAP-compliant numbers. It cannot be used to detract from the GAAP numbers. Set out below are overall principles that entities should apply when presenting additional line items, headings, sub-totals and alternative performance measures:
(a) GAAP numbers should be given at least equal prominence to non-GAAP numbers.
(b) Additional line items, sub-totals and columns may be used, but only if they do not detract from the GAAP numbers by introducing bias or by overcrowding the income statement.
(c) Each additional line item or column should contain all the revenue or expenses that relate to the particular line item or column inserted.
(d) Each additional line item or column should contain only revenue or expense that is revenue or expense of the entity itself.
(e) Items may be segregated (for example, by use of columns or sub-totals) where they are different in nature or function from other items in the income statement.
(f) It is generally not permissible to mix natural and functional classifications of expenses where these categories of expenses overlap.
(g) Terms used for additional line items and sub-totals should be defined if they are not terms recognised in IFRS.
(h) Additional line items, columns and sub-totals should only be presented when they are used internally to manage the business.
(i) Various presentations will be acceptable individually, but consideration should be given to the aggregate effect of these presentations, so that the overall message of the income statement is not distorted or confused.
(j) The presentation method should generally be consistent from year to year.
(k) The presentation method should comply with any local regulatory rules.

8. Earnings before interest and tax (EBIT) may be an appropriate sub-heading to show in the income statement. This line item usually distinguishes between the pre-tax profits arising from operating activities and those arising from financing activities.

9. In contrast, a sub-total for earnings before interest, tax, depreciation and amortisation (EBITDA) can only be included as a sub-total where the entity presents its expenses by nature and provided the sub-total does not detract from the GAAP numbers either by implying that EBITDA is the 'real' profit or by overcrowding the income statement so that the reader cannot determine easily the entity's GAAP performance. Where an entity presents its expenses by function, it will not be possible to show depreciation and amortisation as separate line items in arriving at operating profit, because depreciation and amortisation are types of expense, not functions of the business. In this case, EBITDA can only be disclosed by way of supplemental information in a box, in a footnote, in the notes or in the review of operations.

(All amounts in C thousands unless otherwise stated)

Material items of income and expense

1p97

10. When items of income and expense are material, their nature and amount is disclosed separately either in the income statement or in the notes. In the case of IFRS GAAP plc, these disclosures are made in note 6. Some entities provide this information in the income statement in the form of additional analysis boxes or columns. Further discussion is available in PwC's 'IFRS manual of accounting'.

1p85, 97

11. IAS 1 does not provide a specific name for the types of items that should be separately disclosed. Where an entity discloses a separate category of 'exceptional', 'significant' or 'unusual' items either in the income statement or in the notes, the accounting policy note should include a definition of the chosen term. The presentation and definition of these items should be applied consistently from year to year.

Analysis of expenses by nature or function

1p99

12. Where an entity classifies its expenses by nature, it must ensure that each class of expense includes all items related to that class. Material restructuring cost may, for example, include redundancy payments (employee benefit cost), inventory write-downs (changes in inventory) and impairments in property, plant and equipment. It is not normally acceptable to show restructuring costs as a separate line item in an analysis of expenses by nature where there is an overlap with other line items.

13. Entities that classify their expenses by function include the material items within the function to which they relate. In this case, material items can be disclosed as footnotes or in the notes to the financial statements.

Operating profit

1BC56

14. An entity may elect to include a sub-total for its result from operating activities. This is permitted, but management should ensure that the amount disclosed is representative of activities that would normally be considered to be 'operating'. Items that are clearly of an operating nature (for example, inventory write-downs, restructuring and relocation expenses) are not excluded simply because they occur infrequently or are unusual in amount. Nor can expenses be excluded on the grounds that they do not involve cash flows (for example, depreciation or amortisation). As a general rule, operating profit is the subtotal after 'other expenses' – that is, excluding finance costs and the share of profits of equity-accounted investments – although in some circumstances it may be appropriate for the share of profits of equity-accounted investments to be included in operating profit (see paragraph 16 below).

Re-ordering of line items

1p86

15. The line items and descriptions of those items are re-ordered where this is necessary to explain the elements of performance. However, entities are required to make a 'fair presentation' and should not make any changes unless there is a good reason to do so.

16. The share of profit of associates is normally shown after finance costs; this recognises that the share of profits from associates arises from what is essentially an investing activity, rather than part of the group's operating activities. However, where associates (and joint ventures) are an integral vehicle for the conduct of the group's

(All amounts in C thousands unless otherwise stated)

operations and its strategy, it may be more appropriate to show finance costs after the share of profit of associates and joint ventures. In such cases, it may be appropriate either to insert a sub-total 'profit before finance costs' or to include the share of profits from associates and joint ventures in arriving at operating profit (if disclosed). It would not be appropriate to include the share of associates and joint ventures within 'revenue' (and, therefore, within 'gross profit').

17. Finance income cannot be netted against finance costs; it is included in 'other revenue/other income' or shown separately in the income statement. Where finance income is an incidental benefit, it is acceptable to present finance income immediately before finance costs and include a sub-total of 'net finance costs' in the income statement. Where earning interest income is one of the entity's main line of business, it is presented as 'revenue'.

Discontinued operations

1p82(ea), IFRS5p33(a)(b) 18. As stated in paragraph 4(e) above, entities disclose a single amount in the statement of comprehensive income (or separate income statement), comprising the total of discontinued operations. Paragraph 33 of IFRS 5, 'Non-current assets held for sale and discontinued operations', also requires an analysis of this single amount. This analysis may be presented in the notes or in the statement of comprehensive income (separate income statement). If it is presented in the income statement, it should be presented in a section identified as relating to discontinued operations – that is, separate from continuing operations. The analysis is not required for disposal groups that are newly acquired subsidiaries that meet the criteria to be classified as held for sale on acquisition.

Earnings per share

33p66 19. IAS 33, 'Earnings per share', requires an entity to present in the statement of comprehensive income basic and diluted earnings per share (EPS) for profit or loss from continuing operations attributable to the ordinary equity holders of the parent entity and for total profit or loss attributable to the ordinary equity holders of the parent entity for each class of ordinary shares. Basic and diluted EPS are disclosed with equal prominence for all periods presented.

33p67A 20. If an entity presents a separate income statement, basic and diluted earnings per share are presented at the end of that statement.

33p73 21. Earnings per share based on alternative measures of earnings may also be given if considered necessary but should be presented in the notes to the financial statements only.

33p67 22. If diluted EPS is reported for at least one period, it should be reported for all periods presented, even if it equals basic EPS. If basic and diluted EPS are equal, dual presentation can be accomplished in one line in the statement of comprehensive income.

33p68 23. An entity that reports a discontinued operation discloses the basic and diluted amounts per share for the discontinued operation either in the statement of comprehensive income or in the notes to the financial statements.

33p69, 41, 43 24. Basic and diluted EPS are disclosed even if the amounts are negative (that is, a loss per share). However, potential ordinary shares are only dilutive if their

(All amounts in C thousands unless otherwise stated)

conversion would increase the loss per share. If the loss decreases, the shares are anti-dilutive.

33p4
25. When an entity presents both consolidated financial statements and separate financial statements prepared in accordance with IAS 27, 'Consolidated and separate financial statements', the disclosures required by IAS 33 need to be presented only on the basis of the consolidated information. An entity that chooses to disclose EPS based on its separate financial statements presents such EPS information only in its separate statement of comprehensive income.

Components of other comprehensive income

1p7
26. Components of other comprehensive income (OCI) are items of income and expense (including reclassification adjustments) that are not recognised in profit or loss as required or permitted by other IFRSs. They include: changes in the revaluation surplus relating to property, plant and equipment or intangible assets; remeasurements of post employment defined benefit obligations; gains and losses arising from translating the financial statements of a foreign operation; gains and losses on re-measuring available-for-sale financial assets; and the effective portion of gains and losses on hedging instruments in a cash flow hedge.

1p91, 90
27. Entities may present components of other comprehensive income either net of related tax effect or before related tax effects. If an entity choses to present the items net of tax, the amount of income tax relating to each component of OCI, including reclassification adjustments, is disclosed in the notes.

1p92, 94
28. An entity discloses separately any reclassification adjustments relating to components of other comprehensive income either in the statement of comprehensive income or in the notes.

1p7, 95
29. Reclassification adjustments are amounts reclassified to profit or loss in the current period that were recognised in other comprehensive income in the current or previous periods. They arise, for example, on disposal of a foreign operation, on derecognition of an available-for-sale financial asset and when a hedged forecast transaction affects profit or loss.

1p82A
30. IAS 1 has been amended, effective for annual periods beginning on or after 1 July 2012. The amendment requires items of OCI, classified by nature (including share of the other comprehensive income of associates and joint ventures accounted for using the equity method) , to be grouped into those that will be reclassified subsequently to profit or loss when specific conditions are met and those that will not be reclassified to profit or loss. The amendment also requires entities that present items of OCI before related tax effects with the aggregate tax shown separately to allocate the tax between the items that might be reclassified subsequently to the profit or loss section and those that will not be reclassified.

1p107
31. The amount of dividends recognised as distributions to owners during the period and the related amount per share are presented either in the statement of changes in equity or in the notes. Dividends cannot be displayed in the statement of comprehensive income or income statement.

(All amounts in C thousands unless otherwise stated)

Consistency

1p45   32. The presentation and classification of items in the financial statements is retained from one period to the next unless:
   (a) it is apparent, following a significant change in the nature of the entity's operations or a review of its financial statements that another presentation or classification would be more appropriate, addressing the criteria for the selection and application of accounting policies in IAS 8, 'Accounting policies, changes in accounting estimates and errors'; or
   (b) IFRS requires a change in presentation.

Materiality and aggregation

1p29   33. Each material class of similar items is presented separately in the financial statements. Items of a dissimilar nature or function are presented separately unless they are immaterial.

Offsetting

1p32   34. Assets and liabilities, and income and expenses, are not offset unless required or permitted by an IFRS. Examples of income and expenses that are required or permitted to be offset are as follows:

1p34(a)   (a) Gains and losses on the disposal of non-current assets, including investments and operating assets, are reported by deducting from the proceeds on disposal the carrying amount of the asset and related selling expenses.

1p34(b)   (b) Expenditure related to a provision that is recognised in accordance with IAS 37, 'Provisions, contingent liabilities and contingent assets', and reimbursed under a contractual arrangement with a third party (for example, a supplier's warranty agreement) may be netted against the related reimbursement.

1p35   (c) Gains and losses arising from a group of similar transactions are reported on a net basis (for example, foreign exchange gains and losses or gains and losses arising on financial instruments held for trading). However, such gains and losses are reported separately if they are material.

(All amounts in C thousands unless otherwise stated)

Summary

35. The disclosure requirements surrounding components of OCI can be summarised as follows:

Item	Reference	Requirement in standard	Presentation in IFRS GAAP plc
Each component of other comprehensive income recognised during the period, classified by nature and grouped into those that: – will not be reclassified subsequently to profit and loss; and – will be reclassified subsequently to profit and loss.	IAS 1p82A	Statement of comprehensive income	Statement of comprehensive income
Reclassification adjustments during the period relating to components of other comprehensive income	IAS 1p92	Statement of comprehensive income or notes	Note 29
Tax relating to each component of other comprehensive income, including reclassification adjustments	IAS 1p90	Statement of comprehensive income or notes	Note 13
Reconciliation for each component of equity, showing separately: – Profit/loss – Other comprehensive income – Transactions with owners	IAS 1p106(d)	Statement of changes in equity	Statement of changes in equity
For each component of equity, an analysis of other comprehensive income by item	IAS 1p106A	Statement of changes in equity or notes	Note 29

Consolidated balance sheet

(All amounts in C thousands unless otherwise stated)

Consolidated balance sheet

	Note	As at 31 December 2013	2012 Restated	As at 1 January 2012 Restated
1p10(a), 1p38, 1p113 **Assets**				
1p60, 1p66 **Non-current assets**				
1p54(a) Property, plant and equipment	16	155,341	100,233	107,214
1p54(c) Intangible assets	17	26,272	20,700	21,462
1p54(e), 28p38 Investments accounted for using the equity method	12	18,649	17,053	15,940
1p54(o), 1p56 Deferred income tax assets	32	3,546	3,383	2,879
1p54(d), IFRS7p8(d) Available-for-sale financial assets	19	17,420	14,910	13,222
1p54(d), IFRS7p8(a) Derivative financial instruments	20	395	245	187
1p54(h), IFRS7p8(c) Trade and other receivables	21	2,322	1,352	1,106
		223,945	157,876	162,010
1p60, 1p66 **Current assets**				
1p54(g) Inventories	22	24,700	18,182	17,273
1p54(h), IFRS7p8(c) Trade and other receivables	21	19,765	18,330	16,599
1p54(d), IFRS7p8(d) Available-for-sale financial assets	19	1,950	–	–
1p54(d), IFRS7p8(a) Derivative financial instruments	20	1,069	951	980
1p54(d), IFRS7p8(a) Financial assets at fair value through profit or loss	23	11,820	7,972	7,342
1p54(i), IFRS7p8 Cash and cash equivalents (excluding bank overdrafts)	24	17,928	34,062	22,132
		77,232	79,497	64,326
IFRS5p38, 1p54(p) Assets of disposal group classified as held for sale	25	3,333	–	–
		80,565	79,497	64,326
Total assets		304,510	237,373	226,336

(All amounts in C thousands unless otherwise stated)

	Note	As at 31 December 2013	As at 31 December 2012 Restated	As at 1 January 2012 Restated
Equity and liabilities				
1p54(r) **Equity attributable to owners of the parent**				
1p78(e), 1p54(r) Ordinary shares	26	**25,300**	21,000	20,000
1p78(e), 1p55 Share premium	26	**17,144**	10,494	10,424
1p78(e), 1p55 Other reserves	29	**11,612**	7,194	6,364
1p78(e), 1p55 Retained earnings	28	**74,650**	51,985	51,125
		128,706	90,673	87,913
1p54(q) **Non-controlling interests**	12	**7,888**	1,766	1,500
Total equity		**136,594**	92,439	89,413
Liabilities				
1p60, 1p69 **Non-current liabilities**				
1p54(m), IFRS7p8(f), (g) Borrowings	31	**115,121**	96,346	65,784
1p54(m), IFRS7p8(e) Derivative financial instruments	20	**135**	129	130
1p54(o), 1p56 Deferred income tax liabilities	32	**12,370**	9,053	5,926
1p78(d) Post-employment benefits	33	**5,116**	2,611	1,836
1p54(l), 1p78(d) Provisions for other liabilities and charges	34	**316**	274	250
		133,058	108,413	73,926
1p60, 1p69 **Current liabilities**				
1p54(k), IFRS7p8(f) Trade and other payables	30	**16,670**	12,478	11,031
1p54(n) Current income tax liabilities		**2,566**	2,771	7,219
1p54(m), IFRS7p8(f) Borrowings	31	**11,716**	18,258	42,356
1p54(m), IFRS7p8(e) Derivative financial instruments	20	**460**	618	520
1p54(l) Provisions for other liabilities and charges	34	**3,226**	2,396	1,871
		34,638	36,521	62,997
IFRS5p38, 1p54(p) Liabilities of disposal group clasified as held for sale	25	**220**	–	–
		34,858	36,521	62,997
Total liabilities		**167,916**	144,934	136,923
Total equity and liabilities		**304,510**	237,373	226,336

The notes on pages 22 to 150 are an integral part of these consolidated financial statements.

Consolidated balance sheet

(All amounts in C thousands unless otherwise stated)

10p17 The financial statements on pages 1 to 150 were authorised for issue by the board of directors on 24 February 2014 and were signed on its behalf.

CD Suede
Chief Executive

G Wallace
Finance Director

(All amounts in C thousands unless otherwise stated)

Commentary – balance sheet

The commentary that follows explains some of the key requirements in IAS 1, 'Presentation of financial statements', that impact the balance sheet/statement of financial position.

1p10   1. IAS 1 refers to the balance sheet as the 'statement of financial position'. This title is not mandatory, so IFRS GAAP plc has elected to retain the better-known title of 'balance sheet'.

1p54, 55   2. Paragraph 54 of IAS 1 sets out the line items that are, as a minimum, required to be presented in the balance sheet. Additional line items, headings and subtotals are presented in the balance sheet when this presentation is relevant to an understanding of the entity's financial position.

1p77, 78   3. An entity discloses, either in the balance sheet or in the notes, further sub-classifications of the line items presented, classified in a manner appropriate to the entity's operations. The detail provided in sub-classifications depends on the IFRS requirements and on the size, nature and function of the amounts involved.

Current/non-current distinction

1p60   4. An entity presents current and non-current assets and current and non-current liabilities as separate classifications in its balance sheet except when a presentation based on liquidity provides information that is reliable and is more relevant. When that exception applies, all assets and liabilities are presented broadly in order of liquidity.

1p61   5. Whichever method of presentation is adopted, an entity discloses the amount expected to be recovered or settled after more than 12 months for each asset and liability line item that combines amounts expected to be recovered or settled: (a) no more than 12 months after the reporting period, and (b) more than 12 months after the reporting period.

1p66-70   6. Current assets include assets (such as inventories and trade receivables) that are sold, consumed or realised as part of the normal operating cycle even when they are not expected to be realised within 12 months after the reporting period. Some current liabilities, such as trade payables and some accruals for employee and other operating costs, are part of the working capital used in the entity's normal operating cycle. Such operating items are classified as current liabilities even if they are due to be settled more than 12 months after the reporting period.

1p68   7. The operating cycle of an entity is the time between the acquisition of assets for processing and their realisation in the form of cash or cash equivalents. When the entity's normal operating cycle is not clearly identifiable, its duration is assumed to be 12 months.

Consolidated balance sheet

(All amounts in C thousands unless otherwise stated)

1p45

Consistency

8. The presentation and classification of items in the financial statements is retained from one period to the next unless:
   (a) it is apparent, following a significant change in the nature of the entity's operations or a review of its financial statements, that another presentation or classification would be more appropriate according to the criteria for selecting and applying accounting policies in IAS 8, 'Accounting policies, changes in accounting estimates and errors'; or
   (b) an IFRS requires a change in presentation.

Materiality and aggregation

1p29

9. Each material class of similar items is presented separately in the financial statements. Items of a dissimilar nature or function are presented separately unless they are immaterial.

Current and deferred tax assets and liabilities

1p54, 56

10. Current and deferred tax assets and liabilities are presented separately from each other and from other assets and liabilities. When a distinction is made between current and non-current assets and liabilities in the balance sheet, deferred tax assets and liabilities are presented as non-current.

Offsetting

1p32

11. Management should not offset assets and liabilities unless required or permitted to by an IFRS. Measuring assets net of valuation allowances – for example, obsolescence allowances on inventories and doubtful debt allowances on receivables – is not offsetting.

Three balance sheets required in certain circumstances

1p40A-40D

12. If an entity has applied an accounting policy retrospectively, restated items retrospectively or reclassified items in its financial statements, it provides a third balance sheet as at the beginning of the preceding period presented. However, where the retrospective change in policy or the restatement has no effect on this earliest statement of financial position, we believe that it would be sufficient for the entity merely to disclose that fact.

(All amounts in C thousands unless otherwise stated)

Consolidated statement of changes in equity

1p109(c), 1p108, 1p109, 1p113		Notes	Share capital	Share premium	Attributable to owners of the parent			Non-cont-rolling interest	Total equity
					Other reserves[1]	Retained earnings	Total		
1p106(b)	Balance as at 1 January 2012 (as previously reported)		20,000	10,424	6,263	51,456	88,143	1,263	89,406
	Effect of changes in accounting policies	43	–	–	101	(331)	(230)	237	7
	Balance as at 1 January 2012 (restated)		20,000	10,424	6,364	51,125	87,913	1,500	89,413
1p106(d)(i)	Profit for the year		–	–	–	16,304	16,304	856	17,160
1p106(d)(ii)	Other comprehensive income for the year[2]		–	–	830	(550)	280	(40)	240
1p106(a)	Total comprehensive income for the year		–	–	830	15,754	16,584	816	17,400
IFRS2p50	Value of employee services	28	–	–	–	822	822	–	822
	Tax credit relating to share option scheme	28	–	–	–	20	20	–	20
	Proceeds from shares issued	26	1,000	70	–	–	1,070	–	1,070
1p106(d)(iii)	Dividends	34	–	–	–	(15,736)	(15,736)	(550)	(16,286)
1p106(d)(iii)	Total transactions with owners, recognised directly in equity		1,000	70	–	(14,894)	(13,824)	(550)	(14,374)
	Balance as at 31 December 2012 (restated)		21,000	10,494	7,194	51,985	90,673	1,766	92,439
	Balance at 1 January 2013 (restated)		21,000	10,494	7,194	51,985	90,673	1,766	92,439
1p106(d)(i)	Profit for the year		–	–	–	31,874	31,874	2,548	34,422
1p106(d)(ii)	Other comprehensive income for the year[2]		–	–	2,249	173	2,422	252	2,674
1p106(a)	Total comprehensive income for the year		–	–	2,249	32,047	34,296	2,800	37,096

[1] Individual reserves can be grouped into 'other reserves' in the statement of changes in equity if these are similar in nature and can be regarded as a component of equity. If the individual reserves are not shown in the statement of changes in equity, an analysis should be given in the notes.

[2] Companies can implement this by either (a) showing each line item of other comprehensive income separately in the above statement; or (b) having a single-line presentation of other comprehensive income (as shown above) plus a separate note showing an analysis of each item of other comprehensive income for each component of equity.

Consolidated statement of changes in equity

(All amounts in C thousands unless otherwise stated)

			Attributable to owners of the parent					Non-cont-rolling interest	Total equity
		Note	Share capital	Share premium	Other reserves	Retained earnings	Total		
IFRS2p50	Value of employee services	28	–	–	–	690	690	–	690
	Tax credit relating to share option scheme	28	–	–	–	30	30	–	30
	Proceeds from shares issued	26	750	200	–	–	950	–	950
	Purchase of treasury shares	29	–	–	(2,564)	–	(2,564)	–	(2,564)
	Issue of ordinary shares related to business combination	26	3,550	6,450	–	–	10,000	–	10,000
	Convertible bond – equity component	29	–	–	5,433	–	5,433	–	5,433
1p106(d)(iii)	Dividends	34	–	–	–	(10,102)	(10,102)	(1,920)	(12,022)
1p106(d)(iii)	Total contributions by and distributions to owners of the parent, recognised directly in equity		4,300	6,650	2,869	(9,382)	4,437	(1,920)	2,517
1p106(d)(iii)	Non-controlling interest arising on business combination	39	–	–	–	–	–	4,542	4,542
1p106(d)(iii)	Acquisition of non-controlling interest in XYZ Group	40	–	–	(800)	–	(800)	(300)	(1,100)
1p106(d)(iii)	Sale of interest to non-controlling interest in Red Limited	40	–	–	100	–	100	1,000	1,100
1p106(d)(iii)	Total changes in ownership interests in subsidiaries that do not result in a loss of control		–	–	(700)	–	(700)	5,242	4,542
1p106(d)(iii)	Total transactions with owners, recognised directly in equity		4,300	6,650	2,169	(9,382)	3,737	3,322	7,059
	Balance as at 31 December 2013		**25,300**	**17,144**	**11,612**	**74,650**	**128,706**	**7,888**	**136,594**

The notes to pages 22 to 150 are an integral part of these consolidated financial statements.

(All amounts in C thousands unless otherwise stated)

Commentary – statement of changes in equity

The commentary that follows explains some of the key requirements in IAS 1, 'Presentation of financial statements', and other aspects that impact the statement of changes in equity.

Dividends

1p107

1. The amount of dividends recognised as distributions to owners during the period and the related amount per share are presented either in the statement of changes in equity or in the notes. Dividends cannot be displayed in the statement of comprehensive income or income statement.

Non-controlling interest

1p106

2. Information to be included in the statement of changes in equity includes:
  (a) Total comprehensive income for the period, showing separately the total amounts attributable to equity holders of the company and to non-controlling interest.
  (b) For each component of equity, the effects of retrospective application or retrospective restatement recognised in accordance with IAS 8.
  (c) For each component of equity, a reconciliation between the carrying amount at the beginning and the end of the period, separately disclosing changes resulting from:
    (i) profit or loss;
    (ii) other comprehensive income; and
    (iii) transactions with owners in their capacity as owners, showing separately contributions by and distributions to owners and changes in ownership interests in subsidiaries that do not result in loss of control.

3. For each component of equity, the analysis of other comprehensive income by item may be presented either in the statement of changes in equity or disclosed within the notes.

Consolidated statement of cash flows

(All amounts in C thousands unless otherwise stated)

Consolidated statement of cash flows

1p10(d), 7p10, 18(b), 1p38, p113		Note	Year ended 31 December	
			2013	2012 Restated
	Cash flows from operating activities			
	Cash generated from operations	36	**74,751**	41,703
7p31	Interest paid		**(7,835)**	(14,773)
7p35	Income tax paid		**(14,909)**	(10,526)
	Net cash generated from operating activities		**52,007**	16,404
7p21, 7p10	**Cash flows from investing activities**			
7p39	Acquisition of subsidiary, net of cash acquired	39	**(3,750)**	–
7p16(a)	Purchases of property, plant and equipment	16	**(9,505)**	(6,042)
7p16(b)	Proceeds from sale of property, plant and equipment	36	**6,354**	2,979
7p16(a)	Purchases of intangible assets	17	**(3,050)**	(700)
7p16(c)	Purchases of available-for-sale financial assets	19	**(4,887)**	(1,150)
	Proceeds from disposal of available-for-sale financial assets		**151**	–
7p16(e)	Loans granted to related parties	41	**(1,343)**	(112)
7p16(f)	Loan repayments received from related parties	41	**63**	98
7p31	Interest received		**1,054**	1,193
7p31	Dividends received		**1,130**	1,120
	Net cash used in investing activities		**(13,783)**	(2,614)

(All amounts in C thousands unless otherwise stated)

	Note	Year ended 31 December	
		2013	2012 Restated
7p21, 7p10 **Cash flows from financing activities**			
7p17(a) Proceeds from issuance of ordinary shares	26	950	1,070
7p17(b) Purchase of treasury shares		(2,564)	–
7p17(c) Proceeds from issuance of convertible bonds	31	50,000	–
7p17(c) Proceeds from issuance of redeemable preference shares	31	–	30,000
7p17(c) Proceeds from borrowings		8,500	18,000
7p17(d) Repayments of borrowings		(93,993)	(34,674)
7p31 Dividends paid to owners of the parent	31	(10,102)	(15,736)
7p31 Dividends paid to holders of redeemable preference shares		(1,950)	(1,950)
Acquisition of interest in a subsidiary		(1,100)	–
Sale of interest in a subsidiary		1,100	–
7p31 Dividends paid to non-controlling interests		(1,920)	(550)
Net cash used in financing activities		**(51,079)**	(3,840)
Net (decrease)/increase in cash and cash equivalents		**(12,855)**	9,950
7p28 Cash and cash equivalents at beginning of year	24	27,598	17,587
Exchange gains/(losses) on cash and cash equivalents		535	61
7p28 **Cash and cash equivalents at end of year**	24	**15,278**	27,598

The notes on pages 22 to 150 are an integral part of these consolidated financial statements.

Consolidated statement of cash flows

(All amounts in C thousands unless otherwise stated)

(All amounts in C thousands unless otherwise stated)

(c) cash advances and loans made to customers and the repayment of those advances and loans.

Interest and dividends

7p31   7. Cash flows from interest and dividends received and paid are each disclosed separately. Each is classified in a consistent manner from period to period as either operating, investing or financing activities.

7p33   8. Interest paid and interest and dividends received are usually classified as operating cash flows for a financial institution. However, there is no consensus on the classification of these cash flows for other entities. Interest paid and interest and dividends received may be classified as operating cash flows because they enter into the determination of net profit or loss. Alternatively, interest paid and interest and dividends received may be classified as financing cash flows and investing cash flows respectively, because they are costs of obtaining financial resources or returns on investments.

7p34   9. Dividends paid may be classified as financing cash flows because they are a cost of obtaining financial resources. Alternatively, they may be classified as operating cash flows to assist users to determine the ability of an entity to pay dividends out of operating cash flows.

Income taxes

7p35   10. Cash flows arising from income taxes are separately disclosed and classified as cash flows from operating activities unless they can be specifically identified with financing and investing activities.

Effects of exchange rate changes

7p28   11. Unrealised gains and losses arising from changes in foreign currency exchange rates are not cash flows. However, the effect of exchange rate changes on cash and cash equivalents held or due in a foreign currency are reported in the statement of cash flows in order to reconcile cash and cash equivalents at the beginning and the end of the period. This amount is presented separately from cash flows from operating, investing and financing activities. It also includes the differences, if any, had those cash flows been reported at period-end exchange rates.

Additional recommended disclosures

7p50   12. Additional information may be relevant to users in understanding the financial position and liquidity of an entity. Disclosure of this information, together with a commentary by management, is encouraged and may include:

7p50(a)   (a) The amount of undrawn borrowing facilities that may be available for future operating activities and to settle capital commitments, indicating any restrictions on the use of these facilities.

7p50(c)   (b) The aggregate amount of cash flows that represent increases in operating capacity separately from those cash flows that are required to maintain operating capacity.

7p50(d)   (c) The amount of the cash flows arising from the operating, investing and financing activities of each reportable segment (see IFRS 8, 'Operating segments').

(All amounts in C thousands unless otherwise stated)

Notes to the consolidated financial statements

1 General information

1p138(b)-(c), 1p51(a)(b)	IFRS GAAP plc ('the company') and its subsidiaries (together, 'the group') manufacture, distribute and sell shoes through a network of independent retailers. The group has manufacturing plants around the world and sells mainly in countries within the UK, the US, Europe and Russia. During the year, the group acquired control of 'ABC Group', a shoe and leather goods retailer operating in the US and most western European countries.
1p138(a)	The company is a public limited company, which is listed on the EuroMoney Stock Exchange and incorporated and domiciled in One-Land. The address of its registered office is Nice Walk Way, One-Land.

2 Summary of significant accounting policies

> ## PwC Commentary
>
> The following note is a complete reiteration of a large number of possible accounting policies. Management should only present information that relates directly to the business and should avoid boilerplate disclosure.

1p112(a), 1p117(b), 1p119	The principal accounting policies applied in the preparation of these consolidated financial statements are set out below. These policies have been consistently applied to all the years presented, unless otherwise stated.

2.1 Basis of preparation

1p116, 1p117(a)	The consolidated financial statements of IFRS GAAP plc have been prepared in accordance with International Financial Reporting Standards (IFRS) and IFRS Interpretations Committee (IFRS IC) applicable to companies reporting under IFRS. The consolidated financial statements have been prepared under the historical cost convention, as modified by the revaluation of land and buildings, available-for-sale financial assets, and financial assets and financial liabilities (including derivative instruments) at fair value through profit or loss.

The preparation of financial statements in conformity with IFRS requires the use of certain critical accounting estimates. It also requires management to exercise its judgement in the process of applying the group's accounting policies. The areas involving a higher degree of judgement or complexity, or areas where assumptions and estimates are significant to the consolidated financial statements are disclosed in note 4.

(All amounts in C thousands unless otherwise stated)

2.1.1 Changes in accounting policy and disclosures[1]

8p28

New and amended standards adopted by the group

The following standards have been adopted by the group for the first time for the financial year beginning on or after 1 January 2013 and have a material impact on the group:

Amendment to IAS 1, 'Financial statement presentation' regarding other comprehensive income. The main change resulting from these amendments is a requirement for entities to group items presented in 'other comprehensive income' (OCI) on the basis of whether they are potentially reclassifiable to profit or loss subsequently (reclassification adjustments).

IAS 19, 'Employee benefits' was revised in June 2011. The changes on the group's accounting policies has been as follows: to immediately recognise all past service costs; and to replace interest cost and expected return on plan assets with a net interest amount that is calculated by applying the discount rate to the net defined benefit liability (asset). See note 43 for the impact on the financial statements.

Amendment to IFRS 7, 'Financial instruments: Disclosures', on asset and liability offsetting. This amendment includes new disclosures to facilitate comparison between those entities that prepare IFRS financial statements to those that prepare financial statements in accordance with US GAAP.

IFRS 10, 'Consolidated financial statements' builds on existing principles by identifying the concept of control as the determining factor in whether an entity should be included within the consolidated financial statements of the parent company. The standard provides additional guidance to assist in the determination of control where this is difficult to assess. See note 43 for the impact on the financial statements.

IFRS 11, 'Joint arrangements' focuses on the rights and obligations of the parties to the arrangement rather than its legal form. There are two types of joint arrangements: joint operations and joint ventures. Joint operations arise where the investors have rights to the assets and obligations for the liabilities of an arrangement. A joint operator accounts for its share of the assets, liabilities, revenue and expenses. Joint ventures arise where the investors have rights to the net assets of the arrangement; joint ventures are accounted for under the equity method. Proportional consolidation of joint arrangements is no longer permitted. See note 43 for the impact of adoption on the financial statements.

IFRS 12, 'Disclosures of interests in other entities' includes the disclosure requirements for all forms of interests in other entities, including joint arrangements, associates, structured entities and other off balance sheet vehicles.

IFRS 13, 'Fair value measurement', aims to improve consistency and reduce complexity by providing a precise definition of fair value and a single source of fair value measurement and disclosure requirements for use across IFRSs. The requirements, which are largely aligned between IFRSs and US GAAP, do not extend the use of fair value accounting but provide guidance on how it should be applied where its use is already required or permitted by other standards within IFRSs.

---

[1] A detailed list of IFRSs and IFRIC interpretations effective on or after 1 January 2013 is included as Appendix IV.

(All amounts in C thousands unless otherwise stated)

Amendments to IAS 36, 'Impairment of assets', on the recoverable amount disclosures for non-financial assets. This amendment removed certain disclosures of the recoverable amount of CGUs which had been included in IAS 36 by the issue of IFRS 13. The amendment is not mandatory for the group until 1 January 2014, however the group has decided to early adopt the amendment as of 1 January 2013.

New standards and interpretations not yet adopted

8p30,31 A number of new standards and amendments to standards and interpretations are effective for annual periods beginning after 1 January 2013, and have not been applied in preparing these consolidated financial statement. None of these is expected to have a significant effect on the consolidated financial statements of the Group, except the following set out below:

IFRS 9, 'Financial instruments', addresses the classification, measurement and recognition of financial assets and financial liabilities. IFRS 9 was issued in November 2009 and October 2010. It replaces the parts of IAS 39 that relate to the classification and measurement of financial instruments. IFRS 9 requires financial assets to be classified into two measurement categories: those measured as at fair value and those measured at amortised cost. The determination is made at initial recognition. The classification depends on the entity's business model for managing its financial instruments and the contractual cash flow characteristics of the instrument. For financial liabilities, the standard retains most of the IAS 39 requirements. The main change is that, in cases where the fair value option is taken for financial liabilities, the part of a fair value change due to an entity's own credit risk is recorded in other comprehensive income rather than the income statement, unless this creates an accounting mismatch. The group is yet to assess IFRS 9's full impact. The Group will also consider the impact of the remaining phases of IFRS 9 when completed by the Board.

IFRIC 21, 'Levies', sets out the accounting for an obligation to pay a levy that is not income tax. The interpretation addresses what the obligating event is that gives rise to pay a levy and when should a liability be recognised. The Group is not currently subjected to significant levies so the impact on the Group is not material.

There are no other IFRSs or IFRIC interpretations that are not yet effective that would be expected to have a material impact on the Group.

1p119 **2.2 Consolidation**

(a) Subsidiaries

IFRS10p7, Subsidiaries are all entities (including structured entities) over which the group has
IFRS10p20, control. The group controls an entity when the group is exposed to, or has rights to,
IFRS10p25 variable returns from its involvement with the entity and has the ability to affect those returns through its power over the entity. Subsidiaries are fully consolidated from the date on which control is transferred to the group. They are deconsolidated from the date that control ceases.

IFRS3p5, The group applies the acquisition method to account for business combinations. The
IFRS3p37, consideration transferred for the acquisition of a subsidiary is the fair values of the
IFRS3p39, assets transferred, the liabilities incurred to the former owners of the acquiree and
IFRS3p18, the equity interests issued by the group. The consideration transferred includes the
IFRS3p19

(All amounts in C thousands unless otherwise stated)

fair value of any asset or liability resulting from a contingent consideration arrangement. Identifiable assets acquired and liabilities and contingent liabilities assumed in a business combination are measured initially at their fair values at the acquisition date. The group recognises any non-controlling interest in the acquiree on an acquisition-by-acquisition basis, either at fair value or at the non-controlling interest's proportionate share of the recognised amounts of acquiree's identifiable net assets.

IFRS3p53   Acquisition-related costs are expensed as incurred.

IFRS3p42   If the business combination is achieved in stages, the acquisition date carrying value of the acquirer's previously held equity interest in the acquiree is re-measured to fair value at the acquisition date; any gains or losses arising from such re-measurement are recognised in profit or loss.

IFRS3p58   Any contingent consideration to be transferred by the group is recognised at fair value at the acquisition date. Subsequent changes to the fair value of the contingent consideration that is deemed to be an asset or liability is recognised in accordance with IAS 39 either in profit or loss or as a change to other comprehensive income. Contingent consideration that is classified as equity is not re-measured, and its subsequent settlement is accounted for within equity.

IFRS3p32, IFRS3B63(a), 36p80   The excess of the consideration transferred, the amount of any non-controlling interest in the acquiree and the acquisition-date fair value of any previous equity interest in the acquiree over the fair value of the identifiable net assets acquired is recorded as goodwill. If the total of consideration transferred, non-controlling interest recognised and eviously held interest measured is less than the fair value of the net assets of the subsidiary acquired in the case of a bargain purchase, the difference is recognised directly in the income statement (note 2.6).

Inter-company transactions, balances and unrealised gains on transactions between group companies are eliminated. Unrealised losses are also eliminated. When necessary amounts reported by subsidiaries have been adjusted to conform with the group's accounting policies.

(b) Changes in ownership interests in subsidiaries without change of control

IFRS10p23   Transactions with non-controlling interests that do not result in loss of control are accounted for as equity transactions – that is, as transactions with the owners in their capacity as owners. The difference between fair value of any consideration paid and the relevant share acquired of the carrying value of net assets of the subsidiary is recorded in equity. Gains or losses on disposals to non-controlling interests are also recorded in equity.

(c) Disposal of subsidiaries

IFRS10p25, IFRS10pB98, IFRS10pB99   When the group ceases to have control any retained interest in the entity is re-measured to its fair value at the date when control is lost, with the change in carrying amount recognised in profit or loss. The fair value is the initial carrying amount for the purposes of subsequently accounting for the retained interest as an associate, joint venture or financial asset. In addition, any amounts previously recognised in other comprehensive income in respect of that entity are accounted for as if the group had directly disposed of the related assets or liabilities. This may mean that amounts previously recognised in other comprehensive income are reclassified to profit or loss.

Notes to the consolidated financial statements

(All amounts in C thousands unless otherwise stated)

<table>
<tr><td>1p119</td><td>(d) Associates</td></tr>
<tr><td>28p5,28p10</td><td>Associates are all entities over which the group has significant influence but not control, generally accompanying a shareholding of between 20% and 50% of the voting rights. Investments in associates are accounted for using the equity method of accounting. Under the equity method, the investment is initially recognised at cost, and the carrying amount is increased or decreased to recognise the investor's share of the profit or loss of the investee after the date of acquisition. The group's investment in associates includes goodwill identified on acquisition.</td></tr>
<tr><td>28p25</td><td>If the ownership interest in an associate is reduced but significant influence is retained, only a proportionate share of the amounts previously recognised in other comprehensive income is reclassified to profit or loss where appropriate.</td></tr>
<tr><td>28p38,28p39</td><td>The group's share of post-acquisition profit or loss is recognised in the income statement, and its share of post-acquisition movements in other comprehensive income is recognised in other comprehensive income with a corresponding adjustment to the carrying amount of the investment. When the group's share of losses in an associate equals or exceeds its interest in the associate, including any other unsecured receivables, the group does not recognise further losses, unless it has incurred legal or constructive obligations or made payments on behalf of the associate.</td></tr>
<tr><td>28p40,28p42</td><td>The group determines at each reporting date whether there is any objective evidence that the investment in the associate is impaired. If this is the case, the group calculates the amount of impairment as the difference between the recoverable amount of the associate and its carrying value and recognises the amount adjacent to 'share of profit/(loss) of associates in the income statement.</td></tr>
<tr><td>28p28,28p34</td><td>Profits and losses resulting from upstream and downstream transactions between the group and its associate are recognised in the group's financial statements only to the extent of unrelated investor's interests in the associates. Unrealised losses are eliminated unless the transaction provides evidence of an impairment of the asset transferred. Accounting policies of associates have been changed where necessary to ensure consistency with the policies adopted by the group.</td></tr>
<tr><td></td><td>Dilution gains and losses arising in investments in associates are recognised in the income statement.</td></tr>
</table>

(e) Joint arrangements

The group has applied IFRS 11 to all joint arrangements as of 1 January 2012. Under IFRS 11 investments in joint arrangements are classified as either joint operations or joint ventures depending on the contractual rights and obligations each investor. IFRS GAAP plc has assessed the nature of its joint arrangements and determined them to be joint ventures. Joint ventures are accounted for using the equity method.

28p10   Under the equity method of accounting, interests in joint ventures are initially recognised at cost and adjusted thereafter to recognise the group's share of the post-acquisition profits or losses and movements in other comprehensive income. When the group's share of losses in a joint venture equals or exceeds its interests in the joint ventures (which includes any long-term interests that, in substance, form part of the group's net investment in the joint ventures), the group does not recognise further losses, unless it has incurred obligations or made payments on behalf of the joint ventures.

(All amounts in C thousands unless otherwise stated)

IFRS11pC2-3 28p28 Unrealised gains on transactions between the group and its joint ventures are eliminated to the extent of the group's interest in the joint ventures. Unrealised losses are also eliminated unless the transaction provides evidence of an impairment of the asset transferred. Accounting policies of the joint ventures have been changed where necessary to ensure consistency with the policies adopted by the group. The change in accounting policy has been applied as from 1 January 2012.

The effects of the change in accounting policies on the financial position, comprehensive income and the cash flows of the group at 1 January 2012 and 31 December 2012 are shown in note 43. The change in accounting policy has had no impact on earnings per share.

1p119 **2.3 Segment reporting**

IFRS8p5(b) Operating segments are reported in a manner consistent with the internal reporting provided to the chief operating decision-maker. The chief operating decision-maker, who is responsible for allocating resources and assessing performance of the operating segments, has been identified as the steering committee that makes strategic decisions.

1p119 **2.4 Foreign currency translation**

1p119 *(a) Functional and presentation currency*

21p17, 21p9, 18, 1p51(d) Items included in the financial statements of each of the group's entities are measured using the currency of the primary economic environment in which the entity operates ('the functional currency'). The consolidated financial statements are presented in 'currency' (C), which is the group's presentation currency.

1p119 *(b) Transactions and balances*

21p21, 28, 21p32, 39p95(a), 39p102(a) Foreign currency transactions are translated into the functional currency using the exchange rates prevailing at the dates of the transactions or valuation where items are re-measured. Foreign exchange gains and losses resulting from the settlement of such transactions and from the translation at year-end exchange rates of monetary assets and liabilities denominated in foreign currencies are recognised in the income statement, except when deferred in other comprehensive income as qualifying cash flow hedges and qualifying net investment hedges. Foreign exchange gains and losses that relate to borrowings and cash and cash equivalents are presented in the income statement within 'finance income or costs'. All other foreign exchange gains and losses are presented in the income statement within 'Other (losses)/gains – net'.

39AG83 Changes in the fair value of monetary securities denominated in foreign currency classified as available for sale are analysed between translation differences resulting from changes in the amortised cost of the security and other changes in the carrying amount of the security. Translation differences related to changes in amortised cost are recognised in profit or loss, and other changes in carrying amount are recognised in other comprehensive income.

21p30 Translation differences on non-monetary financial assets and liabilities such as equities held at fair value through profit or loss are recognised in profit or loss as part of the fair value gain or loss. Translation differences on non-monetary financial assets, such as equities classified as available for sale, are included in other comprehensive income.

Notes to the consolidated financial statements

(All amounts in C thousands unless otherwise stated)

<table>
<tr><td>1p119</td><td colspan="2">(c) Group companies</td></tr>
<tr><td>21p39</td><td colspan="2">The results and financial position of all the group entities (none of which has the currency of a hyper-inflationary economy) that have a functional currency different from the presentation currency are translated into the presentation currency as follows:</td></tr>
<tr><td>21p39(a)</td><td>(a)</td><td>assets and liabilities for each balance sheet presented are translated at the closing rate at the date of that balance sheet;</td></tr>
<tr><td>21p39(b)</td><td>(b)</td><td>income and expenses for each income statement are translated at average exchange rates (unless this average is not a reasonable approximation of the cumulative effect of the rates prevailing on the transaction dates, in which case income and expenses are translated at the rate on the dates of the transactions); and</td></tr>
<tr><td>1p79(b),
21p39(c)</td><td>(c)</td><td>all resulting exchange differences are recognised in other comprehensive income.</td></tr>
</table>

21p47   Goodwill and fair value adjustments arising on the acquisition of a foreign entity are treated as assets and liabilities of the foreign entity and translated at the closing rate. Exchange differences arising are recognised in other comprehensive income.

1p119   **2.5 Property, plant and equipment**

16p73(a),
16p35(b),
16p15, 16p17,
39p98(b)   Land and buildings comprise mainly factories, retail outlets and offices. Land and buildings are shown at fair value, based on valuations by external independent valuers, less subsequent depreciation for buildings. Valuations are performed with sufficient regularity to ensure that the fair value of a revalued asset does not differ materially from its carrying amount. Any accumulated depreciation at the date of revaluation is eliminated against the gross carrying amount of the asset, and the net amount is restated to the revalued amount of the asset. All other property, plant and equipment is stated at historical cost less depreciation. Historical cost includes expenditure that is directly attributable to the acquisition of the items. Cost may also include transfers from equity of any gains/losses on qualifying cash flow hedges of foreign currency purchases of property, plant and equipment.

16p12   Subsequent costs are included in the asset's carrying amount or recognised as a separate asset, as appropriate, only when it is probable that future economic benefits associated with the item will flow to the group and the cost of the item can be measured reliably. The carrying amount of the replaced part is derecognised. All other repairs and maintenance are charged to the income statement during the financial period in which they are incurred.

16p39, 1p79(b),
16p40, 16p41   Increases in the carrying amount arising on revaluation of land and buildings are credited to other comprehensive income and shown as other reserves in shareholders' equity. Decreases that offset previous increases of the same asset are charged in other comprehensive income and debited against other reserves directly in equity; all other decreases are charged to the income statement. Each year the difference between depreciation based on the revalued carrying amount of the asset charged to the income statement, and depreciation based on the asset's original cost is transferred from 'other reserves' to 'retained earnings'.

(All amounts in C thousands unless otherwise stated)

16p73(b), 50,16p73(c)	Land is not depreciated. Depreciation on other assets is calculated using the straight-line method to allocate their cost or revalued amounts to their residual values over their estimated useful lives, as follows:

- Buildings   25-40 years
- Machinery   10-15 years
- Vehicles   3-5 years
- Furniture, fittings and equipment   3-8 years

16p51   The assets' residual values and useful lives are reviewed, and adjusted if appropriate, at the end of each reporting period.

36p59   An asset's carrying amount is written down immediately to its recoverable amount if the asset's carrying amount is greater than its estimated recoverable amount (note 2.7).

16p68, 71   Gains and losses on disposals are determined by comparing the proceeds with the carrying amount and are recognised within 'Other (losses)/gains – net' in the income statement.

16p41, 1p79(b) When revalued assets are sold, the amounts included in other reserves are transferred to retained earnings.

2.6 Intangible assets

1p119   *(a) Goodwill*

IFRS3p51,
38p108(a),
IFRS3p54,
36p124   Goodwill arises on the acquisition of subsidiaries and represents the excess of the consideration transferred over IFRS GAAP Plc's interest in net fair value of the net identifiable assets, liabilities and contingent liabilities of the acquiree and the fair value of the non-controlling interest in the acquiree.

For the purpose of impairment testing, goodwill acquired in a business combination is allocated to each of the CGUs, or groups of CGUs, that is expected to benefit from the synergies of the combination. Each unit or group of units to which the goodwill is allocated represents the lowest level within the entity at which the goodwill is monitored for internal management purposes. Goodwill is monitored at the operating segment level.

Goodwill impairment reviews are undertaken annually or more frequently if events or changes in circumstances indicate a potential impairment. The carrying value of goodwill is compared to the recoverable amount, which is the higher of value in use and the fair value less costs of disposal. Any impairment is recognised immediately as an expense and is not subsequently reversed.

1p119   *(b) Trademarks and licences*

38p74, 38p97,
38p118(a), (b)   Separately acquired trademarks and licences are shown at historical cost. Trademarks and licences acquired in a business combination are recognised at fair value at the acquisition date. Trademarks and licences have a finite useful life and are carried at cost less accumulated amortisation. Amortisation is calculated using the straight-line method to allocate the cost of trademarks and licences over their estimated useful lives of 15 to 20 years.

Notes to the consolidated financial statements

(All amounts in C thousands unless otherwise stated)

38p4,
38p118(a), (b)
Acquired computer software licences are capitalised on the basis of the costs incurred to acquire and bring to use the specific software. These costs are amortised over their estimated useful lives of three to five years.

1p119 *(c) Computer software*

38p57
Costs associated with maintaining computer software programmes are recognised as an expense as incurred. Development costs that are directly attributable to the design and testing of identifiable and unique software products controlled by the group are recognised as intangible assets when the following criteria are met:

- it is technically feasible to complete the software product so that it will be available for use;
- management intends to complete the software product and use or sell it;
- there is an ability to use or sell the software product;
- it can be demonstrated how the software product will generate probable future economic benefits;
- adequate technical, financial and other resources to complete the development and to use or sell the software product are available; and
- the expenditure attributable to the software product during its development can be reliably measured.

38p66
Directly attributable costs that are capitalised as part of the software product include the software development employee costs and an appropriate portion of relevant overheads.

38p68,71
Other development expenditures that do not meet these criteria are recognised as an expense as incurred. Development costs previously recognised as an expense are not recognised as an asset in a subsequent period.

38p97,
38p118(a), (b)
Computer software development costs recognised as assets are amortised over their estimated useful lives, which does not exceed three years.

1p119 **2.7 Impairment of non-financial assets**

36p9,36p10
Intangible assets that have an indefinite useful life or intangible assets not ready to use are not subject to amortisation and are tested annually for impairment. Assets that are subject to amortisation are reviewed for impairment whenever events or changes in circumstances indicate that the carrying amount may not be recoverable. An impairment loss is recognised for the amount by which the asset's carrying amount exceeds its recoverable amount. The recoverable amount is the higher of an asset's fair value less costs of disposal and value in use. For the purposes of assessing impairment, assets are grouped at the lowest levels for which there are largely independent cash inflows (cash-generating units). Prior impairments of non-financial assets (other than goodwill) are reviewed for possible reversal at each reporting date.

1p119 **2.8 Non-current assets (or disposal groups) held for sale**

IFRS5p6, 15
Non-current assets (or disposal groups) are classified as assets held for sale when their carrying amount is to be recovered principally through a sale transaction and a sale is considered highly probable. They are stated at the lower of carrying amount and fair value less costs to sell.

(All amounts in C thousands unless otherwise stated)

1p119   **2.9 Financial assets**

2.9.1 Classification

IFRS7p21,39p9 The group classifies its financial assets in the following categories: at fair value through profit or loss, loans and receivables, and available for sale. The classification depends on the purpose for which the financial assets were acquired. Management determines the classification of its financial assets at initial recognition.

(a) Financial assets at fair value through profit or loss

39p9   Financial assets at fair value through profit or loss are financial assets held for trading. A financial asset is classified in this category if acquired principally for the purpose of selling in the short term. Derivatives are also categorised as held for trading unless they are designated as hedges. Assets in this category are classified as current assets if expected to be settled within 12 months, otherwise they are classified as non-current.

(b) Loans and receivables

39p9,1p66, 68 Loans and receivables are non-derivative financial assets with fixed or determinable payments that are not quoted in an active market. They are included in current assets, except for maturities greater than 12 months after the end of the reporting period. These are classified as non-current assets. The group's loans and receivables comprise 'trade and other receivables' and 'cash and cash equivalents' in the balance sheet (notes 2.14 and 2.15).

(c) Available-for-sale financial assets

39p9, 1p66, 68, IFRS7 Appx B5(b) Available-for-sale financial assets are non-derivatives that are either designated in this category or not classified in any of the other categories. They are included in non-current assets unless the investment matures or management intends to dispose of it within 12 months of the end of the reporting period.

2.9.2 Recognition and measurement

39p38, IFRS7 AppxB5, 39p43, 39p16, 39p46 Regular purchases and sales of financial assets are recognised on the trade-date – the date on which the group commits to purchase or sell the asset. Investments are initially recognised at fair value plus transaction costs for all financial assets not carried at fair value through profit or loss. Financial assets carried at fair value through profit or loss are initially recognised at fair value, and transaction costs are expensed in the income statement. Financial assets are derecognised when the rights to receive cash flows from the investments have expired or have been transferred and the group has transferred substantially all risks and rewards of ownership. Available-for-sale financial assets and financial assets at fair value through profit or loss are subsequently carried at fair value. Loans and receivables are subsequently carried at amortised cost using the effective interest method.

39p55(a), IFRS7 AppxB5(e) Gains or losses arising from changes in the fair value of the 'financial assets at fair value through profit or loss' category are presented in the income statement within 'Other (losses)/gains – net' in the period in which they arise. Dividend income from financial assets at fair value through profit or loss is recognised in the income statement as part of other income when the group's right to receive payments is established.

Notes to the consolidated financial statements

(All amounts in C thousands unless otherwise stated)

39p55(b), **IFRS7** **AppxB5(e),** **39AG83,** **1p79(b)**	Changes in the fair value of monetary and non-monetary securities classified as available for sale are recognised in other comprehensive income.
39p67	When securities classified as available for sale are sold or impaired, the accumulated fair value adjustments recognised in equity are included in the income statement as 'Gains and losses from investment securities'.
	Interest on available-for-sale securities calculated using the effective interest method is recognised in the income statement as part of other income. Dividends on available-for-sale equity instruments are recognised in the income statement as part of other income when the group's right to receive payments is established.

2.10 Offsetting financial instruments

32p42	Financial assets and liabilities are offset and the net amount reported in the balance sheet when there is a legally enforceable right to offset the recognised amounts and there is an intention to settle on a net basis or realise the asset and settle the liability simultaneously.

2.11 Impairment of financial assets

(a) Assets carried at amortised cost

39p58,39p59	The group assesses at the end of each reporting period whether there is objective evidence that a financial asset or group of financial assets is impaired. A financial asset or a group of financial assets is impaired and impairment losses are incurred only if there is objective evidence of impairment as a result of one or more events that occurred after the initial recognition of the asset (a 'loss event') and that loss event (or events) has an impact on the estimated future cash flows of the financial asset or group of financial assets that can be reliably estimated.
IFRS7B5(f)	Evidence of impairment may include indications that the debtors or a group of debtors is experiencing significant financial difficulty, default or delinquency in interest or principal payments, the probability that they will enter bankruptcy or other financial reorganisation, and where observable data indicate that there is a measurable decrease in the estimated future cash flows, such as changes in arrears or economic conditions that correlate with defaults.
IFRS7p16, **39AG84**	For loans and receivables category, the amount of the loss is measured as the difference between the asset's carrying amount and the present value of estimated future cash flows (excluding future credit losses that have not been incurred) discounted at the financial asset's original effective interest rate. The carrying amount of the asset is reduced and the amount of the loss is recognised in the consolidated income statement. If a loan or held-to-maturity investment has a variable interest rate, the discount rate for measuring any impairment loss is the current effective interest rate determined under the contract. As a practical expedient, the group may measure impairment on the basis of an instrument's fair value using an observable market price.
IFRS7 **AppxB5(d),** **39p65**	If, in a subsequent period, the amount of the impairment loss decreases and the decrease can be related objectively to an event occurring after the impairment was recognised (such as an improvement in the debtor's credit rating), the reversal of the

(All amounts in C thousands unless otherwise stated)

previously recognised impairment loss is recognised in the consolidated income statement.

(b) Assets classified as available for sale

39p67-70   The group assesses at the end of each reporting period whether there is objective evidence that a financial asset or a group of financial assets is impaired. For debt securities, the group uses the criteria referred to in (a) above. In the case of equity investments classified as available for sale, a significant or prolonged decline in the fair value of the security below its cost is also evidence that the assets are impaired. If any such evidence exists for available-for-sale financial assets, the cumulative loss – measured as the difference between the acquisition cost and the current fair value, less any impairment loss on that financial asset previously recognised in profit or loss – is removed from equity and recognised in profit or loss. Impairment losses recognised in the consolidated income statement on equity instruments are not reversed through the consolidated income statement. If, in a subsequent period, the fair value of a debt instrument classified as available for sale increases and the increase can be objectively related to an event occurring after the impairment loss was recognised in profit or loss, the impairment loss is reversed through the consolidated income statement.

1p119   **2.12 Derivative financial instruments and hedging activities**

IFRS7p21,   Derivatives are initially recognised at fair value on the date a derivative contract is
IFRS7p22   entered into and are subsequently re-measured at their fair value. The method of recognising the resulting gain or loss depends on whether the derivative is designated as a hedging instrument, and if so, the nature of the item being hedged. The group designates certain derivatives as either:

(a)   hedges of the fair value of recognised assets or liabilities or a firm commitment (fair value hedge);
(b)   hedges of a particular risk associated with a recognised asset or liability or a highly probable forecast transaction (cash flow hedge); or
(c)   hedges of a net investment in a foreign operation (net investment hedge).

39p88   The group documents at the inception of the transaction the relationship between hedging instruments and hedged items, as well as its risk management objectives and strategy for undertaking various hedging transactions. The group also documents its assessment, both at hedge inception and on an ongoing basis, of whether the derivatives that are used in hedging transactions are highly effective in offsetting changes in fair values or cash flows of hedged items.

IFRS7p23,   The fair values of various derivative instruments used for hedging purposes are
IFRS7p24   disclosed in note 20. Movements on the hedging reserve in other comprehensive income are shown in note 29. The full fair value of a hedging derivative is classified as a non-current asset or liability when the remaining hedged item is more than 12 months, and as a current asset or liability when the remaining maturity of the hedged item is less than 12 months. Trading derivatives are classified as a current asset or liability.

39p89   *(a) Fair value hedge*

Changes in the fair value of derivatives that are designated and qualify as fair value hedges are recorded in the income statement, together with any changes in the fair value of the hedged asset or liability that are attributable to the hedged risk. The

(All amounts in C thousands unless otherwise stated)

group only applies fair value hedge accounting for hedging fixed interest risk on borrowings. The gain or loss relating to the effective portion of interest rate swaps hedging fixed rate borrowings is recognised in the income statement within 'Finance costs'. The gain or loss relating to the ineffective portion is recognised in the income statement within 'Other gains/(losses) – net'. Changes in the fair value of the hedge fixed rate borrowings attributable to interest rate risk are recognised in the income statement within 'Finance costs'.

39p92   If the hedge no longer meets the criteria for hedge accounting, the adjustment to the carrying amount of a hedged item for which the effective interest method is used is amortised to profit or loss over the period to maturity.

39p95   *(b) Cash flow hedge*

1p79(b)   The effective portion of changes in the fair value of derivatives that are designated and qualify as cash flow hedges is recognised in other comprehensive income. The gain or loss relating to the ineffective portion is recognised immediately in the income statement within 'Other gains/(losses) – net'.

39p99, 39p100,   Amounts accumulated in equity are reclassified to profit or loss in the periods when
39p98(b)   the hedged item affects profit or loss (for example, when the forecast sale that is hedged takes place). The gain or loss relating to the effective portion of interest rate swaps hedging variable rate borrowings is recognised in the income statement within 'finance income/cost'. However, when the forecast transaction that is hedged results in the recognition of a non-financial asset (for example, inventory or fixed assets), the gains and losses previously deferred in equity are transferred from equity and included in the initial measurement of the cost of the asset. The deferred amounts are ultimately recognised in cost of goods sold in the case of inventory or in depreciation in the case of fixed assets.

39p101   When a hedging instrument expires or is sold, or when a hedge no longer meets the criteria for hedge accounting, any cumulative gain or loss existing in equity at that time remains in equity and is recognised when the forecast transaction is ultimately recognised in the income statement. When a forecast transaction is no longer expected to occur, the cumulative gain or loss that was reported in equity is immediately transferred to the income statement within 'Other gains/(losses) – net'.

39p102(a)(b)   *(c) Net investment hedge*

Hedges of net investments in foreign operations are accounted for similarly to cash flow hedges.

1p79(b)   Any gain or loss on the hedging instrument relating to the effective portion of the hedge is recognised in other comprehensive income. The gain or loss relating to the ineffective portion is recognised in the income statement. Gains and losses accumulated in equity are included in the income statement when the foreign operation is partially disposed of or sold.

1p119   **2.13 Inventories**

2p36(a),   Inventories are stated at the lower of cost and net realisable value. Cost is
9,2p10,   determined using the first-in, first-out (FIFO) method. The cost of finished goods and
25,23p6,

(All amounts in C thousands unless otherwise stated)

7,2p28, 30,39p98(b)	work in progress comprises design costs, raw materials, direct labour, other direct costs and related production overheads (based on normal operating capacity). It excludes borrowing costs. Net realisable value is the estimated selling price in the ordinary course of business, less applicable variable selling expenses. Costs of inventories include the transfer from equity of any gains/losses on qualifying cash flow hedges for purchases of raw materials[1].

1p119   **2.14 Trade receivables**

IFRS7p21	Trade receivables are amounts due from customers for merchandise sold or services performed in the ordinary course of business. If collection is expected in one year or less (or in the normal operating cycle of the business if longer), they are classified as current assets. If not, they are presented as non-current assets.
39p43, 39p46(a), 39p59, IFRS7 AppxBp5(f), IFRS7 AppxBp5(d)	Trade receivables are recognised initially at fair value and subsequently measured at amortised cost using the effective interest method, less provision for impairment.

1p119   **2.15 Cash and cash equivalents**

IFRS7p21, 7p46	In the consolidated statement of cash flows, cash and cash equivalents includes cash in hand, deposits held at call with banks, other short-term highly liquid investments with original maturities of three months or less and bank overdrafts. In the consolidated balance sheet, bank overdrafts are shown within borrowings in current liabilities.

1p119   **2.16 Share capital**

IFRS7p21, 32p18(a)	Ordinary shares are classified as equity. Mandatorily redeemable preference shares are classified as liabilities (note 2.18).
32p37	Incremental costs directly attributable to the issue of new ordinary shares or options are shown in equity as a deduction, net of tax, from the proceeds.
32p33	Where any group company purchases the company's equity share capital (treasury shares), the consideration paid, including any directly attributable incremental costs (net of income taxes) is deducted from equity attributable to the company's equity holders until the shares are cancelled or reissued. Where such ordinary shares are subsequently reissued, any consideration received, net of any directly attributable incremental transaction costs and the related income tax effects, is included in equity attributable to the company's equity holders.

1p119   **2.17 Trade payables**

Trade payables are obligations to pay for goods or services that have been acquired in the ordinary course of business from suppliers. Accounts payable are classified as current liabilities if payment is due within one year or less (or in the normal operating cycle of the business if longer). If not, they are presented as non-current liabilities.

IFRS7p21, 39p43	Trade payables are recognised initially at fair value and subsequently measured at amortised cost using the effective interest method.

[1] Management may choose to keep these gains in equity until the acquired asset affects profit or loss. At this time, management should re-classify the gains to profit or loss.

Notes to the consolidated financial statements

(All amounts in C thousands unless otherwise stated)

1p119 **2.18 Borrowings**

IFRS7p21 Borrowings are recognised initially at fair value, net of transaction costs incurred. Borrowings are subsequently carried at amortised cost; any difference between the proceeds (net of transaction costs) and the redemption value is recognised in the income statement over the period of the borrowings using the effective interest method.

39p43,39p47 Fees paid on the establishment of loan facilities are recognised as transaction costs of the loan to the extent that it is probable that some or all of the facility will be drawn down. In this case, the fee is deferred until the draw-down occurs. To the extent there is no evidence that it is probable that some or all of the facility will be drawn down, the fee is capitalised as a pre-payment for liquidity services and amortised over the period of the facility to which it relates.

32p18(a), 32p35 Preference shares, which are mandatorily redeemable on a specific date, are classified as liabilities. The dividends on these preference shares are recognised in the income statement as interest expense.

1p119 **2.19 Borrowing costs**

23p8 General and specific borrowing costs directly attributable to the acquisition, construction or production of qualifying assets, which are assets that necessarily take a substantial period of time to get ready for their intended use or sale, are added to the cost of those assets, until such time as the assets are substantially ready for their intended use or sale.

23p12 Investment income earned on the temporary investment of specific borrowings pending their expenditure on qualifying assets is deducted from the borrowing costs eligible for capitalisation.

All other borrowing costs are recognised in profit or loss in the period in which they are incurred.

1p119 **2.20 Compound financial instruments**

32p28 Compound financial instruments issued by the group comprise convertible notes that can be converted to share capital at the option of the holder, and the number of shares to be issued does not vary with changes in their fair value.

32AG31 The liability component of a compound financial instrument is recognised initially at the fair value of a similar liability that does not have an equity conversion option. The equity component is recognised initially at the difference between the fair value of the compound financial instrument as a whole and the fair value of the liability component. Any directly attributable transaction costs are allocated to the liability and equity components in proportion to their initial carrying amounts.

32p36 Subsequent to initial recognition, the liability component of a compound financial instrument is measured at amortised cost using the effective interest method. The equity component of a compound financial instrument is not re-measured subsequent to initial recognition except on conversion or expiry.

1p69, 71 Borrowings are classified as current liabilities unless the group has an unconditional right to defer settlement of the liability for at least 12 months after the end of the reporting period.

(All amounts in C thousands unless otherwise stated)

2.21 Current and deferred income tax

1p119

12p58,12p61A The tax expense for the period comprises current and deferred tax. Tax is recognised in the income statement, except to the extent that it relates to items recognised in other comprehensive income or directly in equity. In this case, the tax is also recognised in other comprehensive income or directly in equity, respectively.

12p12,12p46 The current income tax charge is calculated on the basis of the tax laws enacted or substantively enacted at the balance sheet date in the countries where the company and its subsidiaries operate and generate taxable income. Management periodically evaluates positions taken in tax returns with respect to situations in which applicable tax regulation is subject to interpretation. It establishes provisions where appropriate on the basis of amounts expected to be paid to the tax authorities.

12p24, 12p15, 12p47 Deferred income tax is recognised on temporary differences arising between the tax bases of assets and liabilities and their carrying amounts in the consolidated financial statements. However, deferred tax liabilities are not recognised if they arise from the initial recognition of goodwill; deferred income tax is not accounted for if it arises from initial recognition of an asset or liability in a transaction other than a business combination that at the time of the transaction affects neither accounting nor taxable profit or loss. Deferred income tax is determined using tax rates (and laws) that have been enacted or substantively enacted by the balance sheet date and are expected to apply when the related deferred income tax asset is realised or the deferred income tax liability is settled.

12p24,12p34 Deferred income tax assets are recognised only to the extent that it is probable that future taxable profit will be available against which the temporary differences can be utilised.

12p39, Deferred income tax liabilities are provided on taxable temporary differences arising from investments in subsidiaries, associates and joint arrangements, except for deferred income tax liability where the timing of the reversal of the temporary difference is controlled by the group and it is probable that the temporary difference will not reverse in the foreseeable future. Generally the group is unable to control the reversal of the temporary difference for associates. Only were there is an agreement in place that gives the group the ability to control the reveral of the temporary difference not recognised.

12p44 Deferred income tax assets are recognised on deductible temporary differences arising from investments in subsidiaries, associates and joint arrangements only to the extent that it is probable the temporary difference will reverse in the future and there is sufficient taxable profit available against which the temporary difference can be utilised.

12p74 Deferred income tax assets and liabilities are offset when there is a legally enforceable right to offset current tax assets against current tax liabilities and when the deferred income taxes assets and liabilities relate to income taxes levied by the same taxation authority on either the same taxable entity or different taxable entities where there is an intention to settle the balances on a net basis.

(All amounts in C thousands unless otherwise stated)

2.22 Employee benefits `1p119`

The group operates various post-employment schemes, including both defined benefit and defined contribution pension plans and post-employment medical plans.

(a) Pension obligations

`19Rp26, 19Rp27, 19Rp28` A defined contribution plan is a pension plan under which the group pays fixed contributions into a separate entity. The group has no legal or constructive obligations to pay further contributions if the fund does not hold sufficient assets to pay all employees the benefits relating to employee service in the current and prior periods. A defined benefit plan is a pension plan that is not a defined contribution plan.

`19Rp30` Typically defined benefit plans define an amount of pension benefit that an employee will receive on retirement, usually dependent on one or more factors such as age, years of service and compensation.

`19Rp57, 19Rp58, 19Rp59, 19Rp60, 19Rp67, 19Rp68, 19Rp83` The liability recognised in the balance sheet in respect of defined benefit pension plans is the present value of the defined benefit obligation at the end of the reporting period less the fair value of plan assets. The defined benefit obligation is calculated annually by independent actuaries using the projected unit credit method. The present value of the defined benefit obligation is determined by discounting the estimated future cash outflows using interest rates of high-quality corporate bonds that are denominated in the currency in which the benefits will be paid, and that have terms to maturity approximating to the terms of the related pension obligation. In countries where there is no deep market in such bonds, the market rates on government bonds are used.

`19Rp57(d)` Actuarial gains and losses arising from experience adjustments and changes in actuarial assumptions are charged or credited to equity in other comprehensive income in the period in which they arise.

`19Rp103` Past-service costs are recognised immediately in income.

`19Rp51` For defined contribution plans, the group pays contributions to publicly or privately administered pension insurance plans on a mandatory, contractual or voluntary basis. The group has no further payment obligations once the contributions have been paid. The contributions are recognised as employee benefit expense when they are due. Prepaid contributions are recognised as an asset to the extent that a cash refund or a reduction in the future payments is available.

(b) Other post-employment obligations

`19Rp155` Some group companies provide post-retirement healthcare benefits to their retirees. The entitlement to these benefits is usually conditional on the employee remaining in service up to retirement age and the completion of a minimum service period. The expected costs of these benefits are accrued over the period of employment using the same accounting methodology as used for defined benefit pension plans. Actuarial gains and losses arising from experience adjustments and changes in actuarial assumptions are charged or credited to equity in other comprehensive income in the period in which they arise. These obligations are valued annually by independent qualified actuaries.

(All amounts in C thousands unless otherwise stated)

(c) Termination benefits

19Rp159,

Termination benefits are payable when employment is terminated by the group before the normal retirement date, or whenever an employee accepts voluntary redundancy in exchange for these benefits. The group recognises termination benefits at the earlier of the following dates: (a) when the group can no longer withdraw the offer of those benefits; and (b) when the entity recognises costs for a restructuring that is within the scope of IAS 37 and involves the payment of termination benefits. In the case of an offer made to encourage voluntary redundancy, the termination benefits are measured based on the number of employees expected to accept the offer. Benefits falling due more than 12 months after the end of the reporting period are discounted to their present value.

(d) Profit-sharing and bonus plans

19Rp19

The group recognises a liability and an expense for bonuses and profit-sharing, based on a formula that takes into consideration the profit attributable to the company's shareholders after certain adjustments. The group recognises a provision where contractually obliged or where there is a past practice that has created a constructive obligation.

1p119

2.23 Share-based payments

IFRS2p15(b), IFRS2p19

The group operates a number of equity-settled, share-based compensation plans, under which the entity receives services from employees as consideration for equity instruments (options) of the group. The fair value of the employee services received in exchange for the grant of the options is recognised as an expense. The total amount to be expensed is determined by reference to the fair value of the options granted:

IFRS2p21
- including any market performance conditions (for example, an entity's share price);

IFRS2p20
- excluding the impact of any service and non-market performance vesting conditions (for example, profitability, sales growth targets and remaining an employee of the entity over a specified time period); and

IFRS2p21A
- including the impact of any non-vesting conditions (for example, the requirement for employees to save).

IFRS2p15, IFRS2p20

Non-market performance and service conditions are included in assumptions about the number of options that are expected to vest. The total expense is recognised over the vesting period, which is the period over which all of the specified vesting conditions are to be satisfied.

In addition, in some circumstances employees may provide services in advance of the grant date and therefore the grant date fair value is estimated for the purposes of recognising the expense during the period between service commencement period and grant date.

At the end of each reporting period, the group revises its estimates of the number of options that are expected to vest based on the non-market vesting conditions. It recognises the impact of the revision to original estimates, if any, in the income statement, with a corresponding adjustment to equity.

Notes to the consolidated financial statements

(All amounts in C thousands unless otherwise stated)

When the options are exercised, the company issues new shares. The proceeds received net of any directly attributable transaction costs are credited to share capital (nominal value) and share premium.

The grant by the company of options over its equity instruments to the employees of subsidiary undertakings in the group is treated as a capital contribution. The fair value of employee services received, measured by reference to the grant date fair value, is recognised over the vesting period as an increase to investment in subsidiary undertakings, with a corresponding credit to equity in the parent entity accounts.

The social security contributions payable in connection with the grant of the share options is considered an integral part of the grant itself, and the charge will be treated as a cash-settled transaction.

1p119   **2.24 Provisions**

37p14, 37p72,   Provisions for environmental restoration, restructuring costs and legal claims are
37p63   recognised when: the group has a present legal or constructive obligation as a result of past events; it is probable that an outflow of resources will be required to settle the obligation; and the amount has been reliably estimated. Restructuring provisions comprise lease termination penalties and employee termination payments. Provisions are not recognised for future operating losses.

37p24   Where there are a number of similar obligations, the likelihood that an outflow will be required in settlement is determined by considering the class of obligations as a whole. A provision is recognised even if the likelihood of an outflow with respect to any one item included in the same class of obligations may be small.

37p45   Provisions are measured at the present value of the expenditures expected to be required to settle the obligation using a pre-tax rate that reflects current market assessments of the time value of money and the risks specific to the obligation. The increase in the provision due to passage of time is recognised as interest expense.

1p119   **2.25 Revenue recognition**

18p35(a)   Revenue is measured at the fair value of the consideration received or receivable, and represents amounts receivable for goods supplied, stated net of discounts, returns and value added taxes. The group recognises revenue when the amount of revenue can be reliably measured; when it is probable that future economic benefits will flow to the entity; and when specific criteria have been met for each of the group's activities, as described below. The group bases its estimate of return on historical results, taking into consideration the type of customer, the type of transaction and the specifics of each arrangement.

18p14   *(a) Sales of goods – wholesale*

The group manufactures and sells a range of footwear products in the wholesale market. Sales of goods are recognised when a group entity has delivered products to the wholesaler, the wholesaler has full discretion over the channel and price to sell the products, and there is no unfulfilled obligation that could affect the wholesaler's acceptance of the products. Delivery does not occur until the products have been shipped to the specified location, the risks of obsolescence and loss have been transferred to the wholesaler, and either the wholesaler has accepted the products in

(All amounts in C thousands unless otherwise stated)

accordance with the sales contract, the acceptance provisions have lapsed or the group has objective evidence that all criteria for acceptance have been satisfied.

The footwear products are often sold with volume discounts, customers have a right to return faulty products in the wholesale market. Sales are recorded based on the price specified in the sales contracts, net of the estimated volume discounts and returns at the time of sale. Accumulated experience is used to estimate and provide for the discounts and returns. The volume discounts are assessed based on anticipated annual purchases. No element of financing is deemed present as the sales are made with a credit term of 60 days, which is consistent with the market practice.

18p14   *(b) Sales of goods – retail*

The group operates a chain of retail outlets for selling shoes and other leather products. Sales of goods are recognised when a group entity sells a product to the customer. Retail sales are usually in cash or by credit card.

It is the group's policy to sell its products to the retail customer with a right to return within 28 days. Accumulated experience is used to estimate and provide for such returns at the time of sale. The group does not operate any loyalty programmes.

18p14   *(c) Internet revenue*

Revenue from the provision of the sale of goods on the internet is recognised at the point that the risks and rewards of the inventory have passed to the customer, which is the point of dispatch. Transactions are settled by credit or payment card.

Provisions are made for internet credit notes based on the expected level of returns, which in turn is based upon the historical rate of returns.

18p20   *(d) Sales of services*

The group sells design services and transportation services to other shoe manufacturers. For sales of services, revenue is recognised in the accounting period in which the services are rendered, by reference to stage of completion of the specific transaction and assessed on the basis of the actual service provided as a proportion of the total services to be provided.

18p30(b)   *(e) Royalty income*

Royalty income is recognised on an accruals basis in accordance with the substance of the relevant agreements.

18p30(a)   **2.26 Interest income**

39p63   Interest income is recognised using the effective interest method. When a loan and receivable is impaired, the group reduces the carrying amount to its recoverable amount, being the estimated future cash flow discounted at the original effective interest rate of the instrument, and continues unwinding the discount as interest income. Interest income on impaired loan and receivables is recognised using the original effective interest rate.

Notes to the consolidated financial statements

(All amounts in C thousands unless otherwise stated)

1p119   **2.27 Dividend income**

Dividend income is recognised when the right to receive payment is established.

1p119   **2.28 Leases**

17p33, SIC-15p5   Leases in which a significant portion of the risks and rewards of ownership are retained by the lessor are classified as operating leases. Payments made under operating leases (net of any incentives received from the lessor) are charged to the income statement on a straight-line basis over the period of the lease.

17p27   The group leases certain property, plant and equipment. Leases of property, plant and equipment where the group has substantially all the risks and rewards of ownership are classified as finance leases. Finance leases are capitalised at the lease's commencement at the lower of the fair value of the leased property and the present value of the minimum lease payments.

17p20, 17p27   Each lease payment is allocated between the liability and finance charges. The corresponding rental obligations, net of finance charges, are included in other long-term payables. The interest element of the finance cost is charged to the income statement over the lease period so as to produce a constant periodic rate of interest on the remaining balance of the liability for each period. The property, plant and equipment acquired under finance leases is depreciated over the shorter of the useful life of the asset and the lease term.

1p119   **2.29 Dividend distribution**

10p12   Dividend distribution to the company's shareholders is recognised as a liability in the group's financial statements in the period in which the dividends are approved by the company's shareholders.

1p119   **2.30 Exceptional items**

Exceptional items are disclosed separately in the financial statements where it is necessary to do so to provide further understanding of the financial performance of the group. They are material items of income or expense that have been shown separately due to the significance of their nature or amount.

Commentary – Summary of significant accounting policies

Statement of compliance with IFRS

1p16   1. An entity whose financial statements and notes comply with IFRS makes an explicit and unreserved statement of such compliance in the notes. The financial statements and notes are not described as complying with IFRS unless they comply with all the requirements of IFRS.

2. Where an entity can make the explicit and unreserved statement of compliance in respect of only:
(a)   the parent financial statements and notes, or
(b)   the consolidated financial statements and notes,
it clearly identifies to which financial statements and notes the statement of compliance relates.

(All amounts in C thousands unless otherwise stated)

Summary of accounting policies

1p117(a)
1p117(b)

3. A summary of significant accounting policies includes:
(a) the measurement basis (or bases) used in preparing the financial statements; and
(b) the other accounting policies used that are relevant to an understanding of the financial statements.

1p116

4. The summary may be presented as a separate component of the financial statements.

1p119

5. In deciding whether a particular accounting policy should be disclosed, management considers whether disclosure would assist users in understanding how transactions, other events and conditions are reflected in the reported financial performance and financial position. Some IFRSs specifically require disclosure of particular accounting policies, including choices made by management between different policies they allow. For example, IAS 16, 'Property, plant and equipment', requires disclosure of the measurement bases used for classes of property, plant and equipment.

Changes in accounting policies

Initial application of IFRS

8p28

6. When initial application of an IFRS:
(a) has an effect on the current period or any prior period;
(b) would have such an effect except that it is impracticable to determine the amount of the adjustment; or
(c) might have an effect on future periods, an entity discloses:
   (i) the title of the IFRS;
   (ii) when applicable, that the change in accounting policy is made in accordance with its transitional provisions;
   (iii) the nature of the change in accounting policy;
   (iv) when applicable, a description of the transitional provisions;
   (v) when applicable, the transitional provisions that might have an effect on future periods;
   (vi) for the current period and each prior period presented, to the extent practicable, the amount of the adjustment:
      ■ for each financial statement line item affected;
      ■ if IAS 33, 'Earnings per share', applies to the entity, for basic and diluted earnings per share;
   (vii) the amount of the adjustment relating to periods before those presented, to the extent practicable; and
   (viii) if retrospective application required by paragraph 19(a) or (b) of IAS 8, 'Accounting policies, changes in accounting estimates and errors', is impracticable for a particular prior period, or for periods before those presented, the circumstances that led to the existence of that condition and a description of how and from when the change in accounting policy has been applied.

Financial statements of subsequent periods need not repeat these disclosures.

(All amounts in C thousands unless otherwise stated)

Voluntary change in accounting policy

8p29

7. When a voluntary change in accounting policy:
(a) has an effect on the current period or any prior period,
(b) would have an effect on that period except that it is impracticable to determine the amount of the adjustment, or
(c) might have an effect on future periods,
an entity discloses:
  (i) the nature of the change in accounting policy;
  (ii) the reasons why applying the new accounting policy provides reliable and more relevant information;
  (iii) for the current period and each prior period presented, to the extent practicable, the amount of the adjustment:
    ■ for each financial statement line item affected, and
    ■ if IAS 33 applies to the entity, for basic and diluted earnings per share;
  (iv) the amount of the adjustment relating to periods before those presented, to the extent practicable; and
  (v) if retrospective application is impracticable for a particular prior period, or for periods before those presented, the circumstances that led to the existence of that condition and a description of how and from when the change in accounting policy has been applied.

Financial statements of subsequent periods need not repeat these disclosures.

Change during interim periods

1p112(c)

8. There is no longer an explicit requirement to disclose the financial effect of a change in accounting policy that was made during the final interim period on prior interim financial reports of the current annual reporting period. However, where the impact on prior interim reporting periods is significant, an entity should consider explaining this fact and the financial effect.

IFRSs issued but not yet effective

8p30

9. When an entity has not applied a new IFRS that has been issued but is not yet effective, it discloses:
(a) this fact; and
(b) known or reasonably estimable information relevant to assessing the possible impact that application of the new IFRS will have on the entity's financial statements in the period of initial application.

8p31

10. An entity considers disclosing:
(a) the title of the new IFRS;
(b) the nature of the impending change or changes in accounting policy;
(c) the date by which application of the IFRS is required;
(d) the date as at which it plans to apply it initially; and
(e) either:
  (i) a discussion of the impact that initial application of the IFRS is expected to have on the entity's financial statements, or
  (ii) if that impact is not known or reasonably estimable, a statement to that effect.

11. Our view is that disclosures in the paragraph above are not necessary in respect of standards and interpretations that are clearly not applicable to the entity (for

(All amounts in C thousands unless otherwise stated)

example industry-specific standards) or that are not expected to have a material effect on the entity. Instead, disclosure should be given in respect of the developments that are, or could be, significant to the entity. Management will need to apply judgement in determining whether a standard is expected to have a material effect. The assessment of materiality should consider the impact both on previous transactions and financial position and on reasonably foreseeable future transactions. For pronouncements where there is an option that could have an impact on the entity, the management expectation on whether the entity will use the option should be disclosed.

Disclosures not illustrated in IFRS GAAP plc financial statements

For disclosures relating to IAS 29, 'Financial reporting in hyperinflationary economies', and IFRS 6, 'Exploration for and evaluation of mineral resources', please refer to PricewaterhouseCoopers' *IFRS disclosure checklist 2013*.

3 Financial risk management

3.1 Financial risk factors

IFRS7p31 The group's activities expose it to a variety of financial risks: market risk (including currency risk, fair value interest rate risk, cash flow interest rate risk and price risk), credit risk and liquidity risk. The group's overall risk management programme focuses on the unpredictability of financial markets and seeks to minimise potential adverse effects on the group's financial performance. The group uses derivative financial instruments to hedge certain risk exposures.

Risk management is carried out by a central treasury department (group treasury) under policies approved by the board of directors. Group treasury identifies, evaluates and hedges financial risks in close co-operation with the group's operating units. The board provides written principles for overall risk management, as well as written policies covering specific areas, such as foreign exchange risk, interest rate risk, credit risk, use of derivative financial instruments and non-derivative financial instruments, and investment of excess liquidity.

(a) Market risk

(i) Foreign exchange risk

IFRS7p33(a) The group operates internationally and is exposed to foreign exchange risk arising from various currency exposures, primarily with respect to the US dollar and the UK pound. Foreign exchange risk arises from future commercial transactions, recognised assets and liabilities and net investments in foreign operations.

IFRS7p33(b), IFRS7p22(c) Management has set up a policy to require group companies to manage their foreign exchange risk against their functional currency. The group companies are required to hedge their entire foreign exchange risk exposure with the group treasury. To manage their foreign exchange risk arising from future commercial transactions and recognised assets and liabilities, entities in the group use forward contracts, transacted with group treasury. Foreign exchange risk arises when future commercial transactions or recognised assets or liabilities are denominated in a currency that is not the entity's functional currency.

Notes to the consolidated financial statements

(All amounts in C thousands unless otherwise stated)

IFRS7p22(c)   The group treasury's risk management policy is to hedge between 75% and 100% of anticipated cash flows (mainly export sales and purchase of inventory) in each major foreign currency for the subsequent 12 months. Approximately 90% (2012: 95%) of projected sales in each major currency qualify as 'highly probable' forecast transactions for hedge accounting purposes.

IFRS7 p33(a)(b), IFRS7 p22(c)   The group has certain investments in foreign operations, whose net assets are exposed to foreign currency translation risk. Currency exposure arising from the net assets of the group's foreign operations is managed primarily through borrowings denominated in the relevant foreign currencies.

IFRS7p40, IFRS7IG36   At 31 December 2013, if the currency had weakened/strengthened by 11% against the US dollar with all other variables held constant, post-tax profit for the year would have been C362 (2012: C51) higher/lower, mainly as a result of foreign exchange gains/losses on translation of US dollar-denominated trade receivables, financial assets at fair value through profit or loss, debt securities classified as available-for-sale and foreign exchange losses/gains on translation of US dollar-denominated borrowings. Profit is more sensitive to movement in currency/US dollar exchange rates in 2013 than 2012 because of the increased amount of US dollar-denominated borrowings. Similarly, the impact on equity would have been C6,850 (2012: C6,650) higher/ lower due to an increase in the volume of cash flow hedging in US dollars.

At 31 December 2013, if the currency had weakened/strengthened by 4% against the UK pound with all other variables held constant, post-tax profit for the year would have been C135 (2012: C172) lower/higher, mainly as a result of foreign exchange gains/losses on translation of UK pound-denominated trade receivables, financial assets at fair value through profit or loss, debt securities classified as available-for-sale and foreign exchange losses/gains on translation of UK pound-denominated borrowings.

(ii) Price risk

IFRS7p33(a)(b)   The group is exposed to equity securities price risk because of investments held by the group and classified on the consolidated balance sheet either as available-for-sale or at fair value through profit or loss. The group is not exposed to commodity price risk. To manage its price risk arising from investments in equity securities, the group diversifies its portfolio. Diversification of the portfolio is done in accordance with the limits set by the group.

The group's investments in equity of other entities that are publicly traded are included in one of the following three equity indexes: DAX equity index, Dow Jones equity index and FTSE 100 UK equity index.

IFRS7p40, IFRS7IG36   The table below summarises the impact of increases/decreases of the three equity indexes on the group's post-tax profit for the year and on equity. The analysis is based on the assumption that the equity indexes had increased/decreased by 5% with all other variables held constant and all the group's equity instruments moved according to the historical correlation with the index:

(All amounts in C thousands unless otherwise stated)

	Impact on post-tax profit in C		Impact on other components of equity in C	
	2013	2012	**2013**	2012
Index				
Dax	**200**	120	**290**	290
Dow Jones	**150**	120	**200**	70
FTSE 100 UK	**60**	30	**160**	150

Post-tax profit for the year would increase/decrease as a result of gains/losses on equity securities classified as at fair value through profit or loss. Other components of equity would increase/ decrease as a result of gains/losses on equity securities classified as available for sale.

(iii) Cash flow and fair value interest rate risk

IFRS7p 33(a)(b), IFRSp22(c)
The group's interest rate risk arises from long-term borrowings. Borrowings issued at variable rates expose the group to cash flow interest rate risk which is partially offset by cash held at variable rates. Borrowings issued at fixed rates expose the group to fair value interest rate risk. Group policy is to maintain approximately 60% of its borrowings in fixed rate instruments. During 2013 and 2012, the group's borrowings at variable rate were denominated in the Currency and the UK pound.

IFRS7p22(b)(c) The group analyses its interest rate exposure on a dynamic basis. Various scenarios are simulated taking into consideration refinancing, renewal of existing positions, alternative financing and hedging. Based on these scenarios, the group calculates the impact on profit and loss of a defined interest rate shift. For each simulation, the same interest rate shift is used for all currencies. The scenarios are run only for liabilities that represent the major interest-bearing positions.

Based on the simulations performed, the impact on post tax profit of a 0.1% shift would be a maximum increase of C41 (2012: C37) or decrease of C34 (2012: C29), respectively. The simulation is done on a quarterly basis to verify that the maximum loss potential is within the limit given by the management.

IFRS7p22(b)(c) Based on the various scenarios, the group manages its cash flow interest rate risk by using floating-to-fixed interest rate swaps. Such interest rate swaps have the economic effect of converting borrowings from floating rates to fixed rates. Generally, the group raises long-term borrowings at floating rates and swaps them into fixed rates that are lower than those available if the group borrowed at fixed rates directly. Under the interest rate swaps, the group agrees with other parties to exchange, at specified intervals (primarily quarterly), the difference between fixed contract rates and floating-rate interest amounts calculated by reference to the agreed notional amounts.

IFRS7p22(b)(c) Occasionally the group also enters into fixed-to-floating interest rate swaps to hedge the fair value interest rate risk arising where it has borrowed at fixed rates in excess of the 60% target.

IFRS7p40, IFRS7IG36
At 31 December 2013, if interest rates on Currency-denominated borrowings had been 10 basis points higher/lower with all other variables held constant, post-tax profit for the year would have been C22 (2012: C21) lower/higher, mainly as a result of higher/lower interest expense on floating rate borrowings; other components of equity would have been C5 (2012: C3) lower/ higher mainly as a result of a decrease/ increase in the fair value of fixed rate financial assets classified as available for sale.

Notes to the consolidated financial statements

(All amounts in C thousands unless otherwise stated)

At 31 December 2013, if interest rates on UK pound-denominated borrowings at that date had been 0.5% higher/lower with all other variables held constant, post- tax profit for the year would have been C57 (2012: C38) lower/higher, mainly as a result of higher/lower interest expense on floating rate borrowings; other components of equity would have been C6 (2012: C4) lower/higher mainly as a result of a decrease/ increase in the fair value of fixed rate financial assets classified as available for sale.

(b) Credit risk

IFRS7p 33(a)(b), IFRS7p34(a)

Credit risk is managed on group basis, except for credit risk relating to accounts receivable balances. Each local entity is responsible for managing and analysing the credit risk for each of their new clients before standard payment and delivery terms and conditions are offered. Credit risk arises from cash and cash equivalents, derivative financial instruments and deposits with banks and financial institutions, as well as credit exposures to wholesale and retail customers, including outstanding receivables and committed transactions. For banks and financial institutions, only independently rated parties with a minimum rating of 'A' are accepted. If wholesale customers are independently rated, these ratings are used. If there is no independent rating, risk control assesses the credit quality of the customer, taking into account its financial position, past experience and other factors. Individual risk limits are set based on internal or external ratings in accordance with limits set by the board. The utilisation of credit limits is regularly monitored. Sales to retail customers are settled in cash or using major credit cards. See notes 18(b) and 21 for further disclosure on credit risk.

No credit limits were exceeded during the reporting period, and management does not expect any losses from non-performance by these counterparties.

(c) Liquidity risk

IFRS7p33(a), (b), IFRS7p34(a)

Cash flow forecasting is performed in the operating entities of the group in and aggregated by group finance. Group finance monitors rolling forecasts of the group's liquidity requirements to ensure it has sufficient cash to meet operational needs while maintaining sufficient headroom on its undrawn committed borrowing facilities (note 31) at all times so that the group does not breach borrowing limits or covenants (where applicable) on any of its borrowing facilities. Such forecasting takes into consideration the group's debt financing plans, covenant compliance, compliance with internal balance sheet ratio targets and, if applicable external regulatory or legal requirements – for example, currency restrictions.

IFRS7p33(a), (b), IFRS7p39(c), IFRS7B11E

Surplus cash held by the operating entities over and above balance required for working capital management are transferred to the group treasury. Group treasury invests surplus cash in interest bearing current accounts, time deposits, money market deposits and marketable securities, choosing instruments with appropriate maturities or sufficient liquidity to provide sufficient headroom as determined by the above-mentioned forecasts. At the reporting date, the group held money market funds of C6, 312 (2012: C934) and other liquid assets of C321 (2012: C1, 400) that are expected to readily generate cash inflows for managing liquidity risk.

IFRS7p39(a)(b) The table below analyses the group's non-derivative financial liabilities and net-settled derivative financial liabilities into relevant maturity groupings based on the remaining period at the balance sheet date to the contractual maturity date. Derivative financial liabilities are included in the analysis if their contractual maturities

(All amounts in C thousands unless otherwise stated)

are essential for an understanding of the timing of the cash flows. The amounts disclosed in the table are the contractual undiscounted cash flows.[1]

At 31 December 2013	Less than 3 month	Between 3 month and 1 year[2]	Between 1 and 2 years[2]	Between 2 and 5 years[2]	Over 5 years[2]
Borrowings (ex finance lease liabilities)	2,112	11,384	25,002	71,457	38,050
Finance lease liabilities	639	2,110	1,573	4,719	2,063
Trading and net settled derivative financial instruments (interest rate swaps)	280	–	10	116	41
Trade and other payables[3]	12,543	3,125	–	–	–
Financial guarantee contracts	21	–	–	–	–
At 31 December 2012					
Borrowings (ex finance lease liabilities)	4,061	12,197	11,575	58,679	38,103
Finance lease liabilities	697	2,506	1,790	5,370	2,891
Trading and net settled derivative financial instruments (interest rate swaps)	317	–	15	81	50
Trade and other payables[3]	9,214	2,304	–	–	–
Financial guarantee contracts	10	–	–	–	–

IFRS7B10A(a) Of the C71,457 disclosed in the 2013 borrowings time band 'Between 2 and 5 years' the company intends to repay C40,000 in the first quarter of 2014 (2012: nil).

IFRS7p39(b) The group's trading portfolio derivative instruments with a negative fair value have been included at their fair value of C 268 (2012: C298) within the less than three month time bucket. This is because the contractual maturities are not essential for an understanding of the timing of the cash flows. These contracts are managed on a net-fair value basis rather than by maturity date. Net settled derivatives comprise interest rate swaps used by the group to manage the group's interest rate profile.

IFRS7p39(b) All of the non-trading group's gross settled derivative financial instruments are in hedge relationships and are due to settle within 12 months of the balance sheet date. These contracts require undiscounted contractual cash inflows of C78,756 (2012: C83,077) and undiscounted contractual cash outflows of C78,241 (2012: C83,366).

---

[1] IFRS7 p39(a)(b) The amounts included in the table are the contractual undiscounted cash flows, except for trading derivatives, which are included at their fair value (see below). As a result, these amounts will not reconcile to the amounts disclosed on the balance sheet except for short-term payables where discounting is not applied. Entities can choose to add a reconciling column and a final total that ties into the balance sheet, if they wish.
[2] The specific time-buckets presented are not mandated by the standard but are based on a choice by management based on how the business is managed. Sufficient time buckets should be provided to give sufficient granularity to provide the reader with an understanding of the entity's liquidity.
[3] The maturity analysis applies to financial instruments only and therefore non-financial liabilities are not included.

Notes to the consolidated financial statements

(All amounts in C thousands unless otherwise stated)

1p134, 1p135, **3.2 Capital management**
IG10

The group's objectives when managing capital are to safeguard the group's ability to continue as a going concern in order to provide returns for shareholders and benefits for other stakeholders and to maintain an optimal capital structure to reduce the cost of capital.

In order to maintain or adjust the capital structure, the group may adjust the amount of dividends paid to shareholders, return capital to shareholders, issue new shares or sell assets to reduce debt.

Consistent with others in the industry, the group monitors capital on the basis of the gearing ratio. This ratio is calculated as net debt divided by total capital. Net debt is calculated as total borrowings (including 'current and non-current borrowings' as shown in the consolidated balance sheet) less cash and cash equivalents. Total capital is calculated as 'equity' as shown in the consolidated balance sheet plus net debt.

During 2013, the group's strategy, which was unchanged from 2012, was to maintain the gearing ratio within 40% to 50% and a BB credit rating. The BB credit rating has been maintained throughout the period. The gearing ratios at 31 December 2013 and 2012 were as follows:

	2013	2012
Total borrowings (note 31)	126,837	114,604
Less: cash and cash equivalents (note 24)	(17,928)	(34,062)
Net debt	108,909	80,542
Total equity	136,594	92,439
Total capital	245,503	172,981
Gearing ratio	44%	47%

The decrease in the gearing ratio during 2013 resulted primarily from the issue of share capital as part of the consideration for the acquisition of a subsidiary (notes 17 and 39).

3.3 Fair value estimation

The table below analyses financial instruments carried at fair value, by valuation method. The different levels have been defined as follows:

IFRS13p76
- Quoted prices (unadjusted) in active markets for identical assets or liabilities (Level 1).

IFRS13p81
- Inputs other than quoted prices included within level 1 that are observable for the asset or liability, either directly (that is, as prices) or indirectly (that is, derived from prices) (Level 2).

IFRS13p86
- Inputs for the asset or liability that are not based on observable market data (that is, unobservable inputs) (Level 3).

(All amounts in C thousands unless otherwise stated)

IFRS13p93(b) The following table presents the group's financial assets and liabilities that are measured at fair value at 31 December 2013. See note 16 for disclosures of the land and buildings that are measured at fair value and note 25 for disclosures of the disposal groups held for sale that are measured at fair value.

Assets	Level 1	Level 2	Level 3	Total
Financial assets at fair value through profit or loss				
Trading derivatives				
– Foreign exchange contracts	–	250	111	361
Trading securities				
– Real estate industry	8,522	–	–	8,522
– Retail industry	3,298	–	–	3,298
Derivatives used for hedging				
– Interest rate contracts	–	408	–	408
– Foreign exchange contracts	–	695	–	695
Available-for-sale financial assets				
Equity securities				
– Real estate industry	13,369	–	–	13,369
– Retail industry	5,366	–	–	5,366
Debt investments				
– Debentures	210	–	–	210
– Preference shares	78	–	–	78
– Debt securities with fixed interest rates	–	347	–	347
Total assets	30,843	1,700	111	32,654

Liabilities	Level 1	Level 2	Level 3	Total
Financial liabilities at fair value through profit or loss				
Trading derivatives				
– Foreign exchange contracts	–	268	–	268
Contingent consideration	–	–	1,500	1,500
Derivatives used for hedging				
– Interest rate contracts	–	147	–	147
– Foreign exchange contracts	–	180	–	180
Total liabilities	–	595	1,500	2,095

(All amounts in C thousands unless otherwise stated)

The following table presents the group's assets and liabilities that are measured at fair value at 31 December 2012.

Assets	Level 1	Level 2	Level 3	Total
Financial assets at fair value through profit or loss				
Trading derivatives				
– Foreign exchange contracts	–	321	–	321
Trading securities				
– Real estate industry	4,348	–	–	4,348
– Retail industry	3,624	–	–	3,624
Derivatives used for hedging				
– Interest rate contracts	–	269	–	269
– Foreign exchange contracts	–	606	–	606
Available-for-sale financial assets				
Equity securities				
– Real estate industry	8,087	–	–	8,087
– Retail industry	6,559	–	–	6,559
Debt investments				
– Debt securities with fixed interest rates	–	264	–	264
Total assets	22,618	1,460	–	24,078

Liabilities	Level 1	Level 2	Level 3	Total
Financial liabilities at fair value through profit or loss				
Trading derivatives				
– Foreign exchange contracts	–	298	–	298
Derivatives used for hedging				
– Interest rate contracts	–	132	–	132
– Foreign exchange contracts	–	317	–	317
Total liabilities	–	747	–	747

IFRS 13p93(c) There were no transfers between levels 1 and 2 during the year.

(a) Financial instruments in level 1

IFRS13 p91 The fair value of financial instruments traded in active markets is based on quoted market prices at the balance sheet date. A market is regarded as active if quoted prices are readily and regularly available from an exchange, dealer, broker, industry group, pricing service, or regulatory agency, and those prices represent actual and regularly occurring market transactions on an arm's length basis. The quoted market price used for financial assets held by the group is the current bid price. These instruments are included in Level 1. Instruments included in Level 1 comprise primarily DAX, FTSE 100 and Dow Jones equity investments classified as trading securities or available for sale.

(b) Financial instruments in level 2

IFRS13p93(d) The fair value of financial instruments that are not traded in an active market (for example, over-the-counter derivatives) is determined by using valuation techniques. These valuation techniques maximise the use of observable market data where it is available and rely as little as possible on entity specific estimates. If all significant inputs required to fair value an instrument are observable, the instrument is included in level 2.

If one or more of the significant inputs is not based on observable market data, the instrument is included in Level 3.

(All amounts in C thousands unless otherwise stated)

Specific valuation techniques used to value financial instruments include:

- Quoted market prices or dealer quotes for similar instruments;
- The fair value of interest rate swaps is calculated as the present value of the estimated future cash flows based on observable yield curves;
- The fair value of forward foreign exchange contracts is determined using forward exchange rates at the balance sheet date, with the resulting value discounted back to present value;
- Other techniques, such as discounted cash flow analysis, are used to determine fair value for the remaining financial instruments.

Note that all of the resulting fair value estimates are included in Level 2 except for certain forward foreign exchange contracts explained below.

(c) Financial instruments in level 3

IFRS13p93(e) The following table presents the changes in Level 3 instruments for the year ended 31 December 2013.

	Contingent consideration in a business combination	Trading derivatives at fair value through profit or loss	Total
Opening balance	–	–	–
Acquisition of ABC Group	1,000	–	1,000
Transfers into Level 3	–	115	115
Gains and losses recognised in profit or loss	500	(4)	496
Closing balance	1,500	111	1,611
IFRS 13p93(e)(i) Total gains or losses for the period included in profit or loss for assets held at the end of the reporting period, under 'Other gains/losses'	500	(4)	496
IFRS 13p93(f) **Change in unrealised gains or losses for the period included in profit or loss for assets held at the end of the reporting period**	500	(4)	496

The following table presents the changes in Level 3 instruments for the year ended 31 December 2012.

	Trading derivatives at fair value through profit or loss	Total
Opening balance	62	62
Settlements	(51)	(51)
Gains and losses recognised in profit or loss	(11)	(11)
Closing balance	–	–
IFRS 13p93(e)(i) Total gains or losses for the period included in profit or loss for assets held at the end of the reporting period, under 'Other gains/losses'	(11)	(11)
IFRS 13p93(f) **Change in unrealised gains or losses for the period included in profit or loss for assets held at the end of the reporting period**	–	–

Notes to the consolidated financial statements

(All amounts in C thousands unless otherwise stated)

See note 39 for disclosures of the measurement of the contingent consideration.

IFRS13
p93(h)(i)
In 2013, the group transferred a held-for-trading forward foreign exchange contract from Level 2 into Level 3. This is because the counterparty for the derivative encountered significant financial difficulties, which resulted in a significant increase to the discount rate due to increased counterparty credit risk, which is not based on observable inputs.

IFRS13
p93(h)(ii)
If the change in the credit default rate would be shifted by +/- 5% the impact on profit or loss would be C20.

3.4 Offsetting financial assets and financial liabilities

(a) Financial assets

IFRS7
p13c
The following financial assets are subject to offsetting, enforceable master netting arrangements and similar agreements.

As at 31 December 2013	Gross amounts of recognised financial assets	Gross amounts of recognised financial liabilities set off in the balance sheet	Net amounts of financial assets presented in the balance sheet	Related amounts not set off in the balance sheet		Net amount
				Financial instruments	Cash collateral received	
Derivative financial assets	1,939	(475)	1,464	(701)	–	763
Cash and cash equivalents	18,953	(1,025)	17,928	(5,033)	–	12,895
Trade receivables	18,645	(580)	18,065	(92)	–	17,973
Total	**39,537**	**(2,080)**	**37,457**	**(5,826)**	**–**	**31,631**

As at 31 December 2012	Gross amounts of recognised financial assets	Gross amounts of recognised financial liabilities set off in the balance sheet	Net amounts of financial assets presented in the balance sheet	Financial instruments	Cash collateral received	Net amount
Derivative financial assets	1,801	(605)	1,196	(535)	–	661
Cash and cash equivalents	34,927	(865)	34,062	(2,905)	–	31,157
Trade receivables	17,172	(70)	17,102	(58)	–	17,044
Total	53,900	(1,540)	52,360	(3,498)	–	48,862

(All amounts in C thousands unless otherwise stated)

(b) Financial liabilities

IFRS7
p13c

The following financial liabilities are subject to offsetting, enforceable master netting arrangements and similar agreements

As at 31 December 2013	Gross amounts of recognised financial liabilities	Gross amounts of recognised financial assets set off in the balance sheet	Net amounts of financial liabilities presented in the balance sheet	Related amounts not set off in the balance sheet		Net amount
				Financial instruments	Cash collateral received	
Derivative financial liabilities	1,070	(475)	595	(276)	–	319
Bank overdrafts	3,675	(1,025)	2,650	–	–	2,650
Trade payables	9,563	(580)	8,983	(62)	–	8,921
Total	**14,308**	**(2,080)**	**12,228**	**(338)**	**–**	**11,890**

As at 31 December 2012	Gross amounts of recognised financial liabilities	Gross amounts of recognised financial assets set off in the balance sheet	Net amounts of financial liabilities presented in the balance sheet	Financial instruments	Cash collateral received	Net amount
Derivative financial liabilities	1,352	(605)	747	(182)	–	565
Bank overdrafts	7,329	(865)	6,464	(2,947)	–	3,517
Trade payables	9,565	(70)	9,495	(28)	–	9,467
Total	**18,246**	**(1,540)**	**16,706**	**(3,157)**	**–**	**13,549**

IFRS7p13C

For the financial assets and liabilities subject to enforceable master netting arrangements or similar arrangements above, each agreement between the Group and the counterparty allows for net settlement of the relevant financial assets and liabilities when both elect to settle on a net basis. In the absence of such an election, financial assets and liabilities will be settled on a gross basis, however, each party to the master netting agreement or similar agreement will have the option to settle all such amounts on a net basis in the event of default of the other party. Per the terms of each agreement, an event of default includes failure by a party to make payment when due; failure by a party to perform any obligation required by the agreement (other than payment) if such failure is not remedied within periods of 30 to 60 days after notice of such failure is given to the party; or bankruptcy.

(All amounts in C thousands unless otherwise stated)

Commentary – disclosure of offsetting of financial assets and financial liabilities

Amendments to IFRS 7, 'Disclosures – Offsetting financial assets and financial liabilities' require additional disclosures to enable users of financial statements to evaluate the effect or the potential effects of netting arrangements, including rights of set-off associated with an entity's recognised financial assets and recognised financial liabilities, on the entity's financial position. The disclosures in these amendments are required for all recognised financial instruments that are set off in accordance with paragraph 42 of IAS 32. These disclosures also apply to recognised financial instruments that are subject to an enforceable master netting arrangement or similar agreements, irrespective of whether they are set off in accordance with paragraph 42 of IAS 32 [IFRS7 paragraph 13A, B40]. The amendments do not provide a definition of "master netting arrangement" however paragraph 50 of IAS 32 identifies the following characteristics, which a master netting arrangement would have:
– provides for a single net settlement of all financial instruments covered by the agreement in the event of default on, or termination of, any one contract.
– used by financial institutions to provide protection against loss in the event of bankruptcy or other circumstances that result in a counterparty being unable to meet its obligations.
– creates a right of set-off that becomes enforceable and affects the realisation or settlement of individual financial assets and financial liabilities only following a specified event of default or in other circumstances not expected to arise in the normal course of business.

Because of the broad scope of the new offsetting requirements, these disclosures are relevant not only to financial institutions but also corporate entities.

Per IFRS 7 paragraphs B51 and B52, entities may group the quantitative disclosures by type of financial instrument or by counterparty. The above example only illustrates the disclosures by type of financial instrument. When disclosure is provided by counterparty, amounts that are individually significant in terms of total counterparty amounts shall be separately disclosed and the remaining individually insignificant counterparty amounts shall be aggregated into one line item.

(All amounts in C thousands unless otherwise stated)

Commentary – financial risk management

Accounting standard for presentation and disclosure of financial instruments

IFRS7p3

1. IFRS 7, 'Financial instruments: Disclosures', applies to all reporting entities and to all types of financial instruments except:

- Those interests in subsidiaries, associates and joint ventures that are accounted for under IAS 27, 'Consolidated and separate financial statements', or IAS 28, 'Investments in associates and joint ventures'. However, entities should apply IFRS 7 to an interest in a subsidiary, associate or joint venture that according to IAS 27 or IAS 28 is accounted for under IAS 39, 'Financial instruments: Recognition and measurement'. Entities should also apply IFRS 7 to all derivatives on interests in subsidiaries, associates or joint ventures unless the derivative meets the definition of an equity instrument in IAS 32.
- Employers' rights and obligations under employee benefit plans, to which IAS 19, 'Employee benefits', applies.
- Insurance contracts as defined in IFRS 4, 'Insurance contracts'. However, IFRS 7 applies to derivatives that are embedded in insurance contracts if IAS 39 requires the entity to account for them separately. It also applies to financial guarantee contracts if the issuer applies IAS 39 in recognising and measuring the contracts.
- Financial instruments, contracts and obligations under share-based payment transactions to which IFRS 2, 'Share-based payment', applies, except for contracts within the scope of paragraphs 5-7 of IAS 39, which are disclosed under IFRS 7.
- From 1 January 2009 puttable financial instruments that are required to be classified as equity instruments in accordance with paragraphs 16A and 16B or 16C and 16D of IAS 32 (revised).

Parent entity disclosures

IFRS7

2. Where applicable, all disclosure requirements outlined in IFRS 7 should be made for both the parent and consolidated entity. The relief from making parent entity disclosures, which was previously available under IAS 30, 'Disclosures in the financial statements of banks and similar financial institutions', and IAS 32, has not been retained in IFRS 7.

Classes of financial instrument

IFRS7p6, B1-B3

3. Where IFRS 7 requires disclosures by class of financial instrument, the entity groups its financial instruments into classes that are appropriate to the nature of the information disclosed and that take into account the characteristics of those financial instruments. The entity should provide sufficient information to permit reconciliation to the line items presented in the balance sheet. Guidance on classes of financial instruments and the level of required disclosures is provided in appendix B of IFRS 7.

Level of detail and selection of assumptions – information through the eyes of management

IFRS7 p34(a)

4. The disclosures in relation to an entity's financial risk management should reflect the information provided internally to key management personnel. As such, the disclosures that will be provided by an entity, their level of detail and the underlying assumptions used will vary greatly from entity to entity. The disclosures in this illustrative financial statement are only one example of the kind of information that

Notes to the consolidated financial statements

(All amounts in C thousands unless otherwise stated)

may be disclosed; the entity should consider carefully what may be appropriate in its individual circumstances.

Nature and extent of risks arising from financial instruments

IFRS7 p31, 32
5. The financial statement should include qualitative and quantitative disclosures that enable users to evaluate the nature and extent of risks arising from financial instruments to which the entity is exposed at the end of the reporting period. These risks typically include, but are not limited to, credit risk, liquidity risk and market risk.

Qualitative disclosures

IFRS7p33
6. An entity should disclose for each type of risk:
(a) the exposures to the risk and how they arise;
(b) the entity's objectives, policies and processes for managing the risk and the methods used to measure the risk; and
(c) any changes in (a) or (b) from the previous period.

Quantitative disclosures

IFRS7 p34(a)(c)
7. An entity should provide for each type of risk, summary quantitative data on risk exposure at the end of the reporting period, based on information provided internally to key management personnel and any concentrations of risk. This information can be presented in narrative form as is done on pages x to x of this publication. Alternatively, entities could provide the data in a table that sets out the impact of each major risk on each type of financial instruments. This table could also be a useful tool for compiling the information that should be disclosed under paragraph 34 of IFRS 7.

IFRS7 p34(b)
8. If not already provided as part of the summary quantitative data, the entity should also provide the information in paragraphs 9-15 below, unless the risk is not material.

Credit risk

IFRS7p36, 37
9. For each class of financial instrument, the entity should disclose:
(a) the maximum exposure to credit risk and any related collateral held;
(b) information about the credit quality of financial assets that are neither past due nor impaired;
(c) the carrying amount of financial assets that would otherwise be past due or impaired whose terms have been renegotiated;
(d) an analysis of the age of financial assets that are past due but not impaired; and
(e) an analysis of financial assets that are individually determined to be impaired including the factors in determining that they are impaired.

Liquidity risk

IFRS7 p34(a), p39
10 Information about liquidity risk shall be provided by way of:
(a) a maturity analysis for non-derivative financial liabilities (including issued financial guarantee contracts) that shows the remaining contractual maturities;
(b) a maturity analysis for derivative financial liabilities (see paragraph 12 below for details); and
(c) a description of how the entity manages the liquidity risk inherent in (a) and (b).

IFRS7B11F
11. In describing how liquidity risk is being managed, an entity should consider discussing whether it:

(All amounts in C thousands unless otherwise stated)

(a) has committed borrowing facilities or other lines of credit that it can access to meet liquidity needs;

(b) holds deposits at central banks to meet liquidity needs;

(c) has very diverse funding sources;

(d) has significant concentrations of liquidity risk in either its assets or its funding sources;

(e) has internal control processes and contingency plans for managing liquidity risk;

(f) has instruments that include accelerated repayment terms (for example, on the downgrade of the entity's credit rating);

(g) has instruments that could require the posting of collateral (for example, margin calls for derivatives);

(h) has instruments that allow the entity to choose whether it settles its financial liabilities by delivering cash (or another financial asset) or by delivering its own shares; and

(i) has instruments that are subject to master netting agreements.

Maturity analysis

IFRS7B11B

12. The maturity analysis for derivative financial liabilities should disclose the remaining contractual maturities if these maturities are essential for an understanding of the timing of the cash flows. For example, this will be the case for interest rate swaps in a cash flow hedge of a variable rate financial asset or liability and for all loan commitments. Where the remaining contractual maturities are not essential for an understanding of the timing of the cash flows, the expected maturities may be disclosed instead.

IFRS7p39, B11D

13. For derivative financial instruments where gross cash flows are exchanged and contractual maturities are essential to understanding, the maturity analysis should disclose the contractual amounts that are to be exchanged on a gross basis. The amount disclosed should be the amount expected to be paid in future periods, determined by reference to the conditions existing at the end of the reporting period. However, IFRS 7 does not specify whether current or forward rates should be used. We therefore recommend that entities explain which approach has been chosen. This approach should be applied consistently.

IFRS7B11

14. The specific time bands presented are not mandated by the standard but are based on what is reported internally to the key management personnel. The entity uses judgement to determine the appropriate number of time bands.

IFRS7B11D

15. If the amounts included in the maturity tables are the contractual undiscounted cash flows, these amounts will not reconcile to the amounts disclosed on the balance sheet for borrowings, derivative financial instruments and trade and other payables. Entities can choose to add a column with the carrying amounts that ties into the balance sheet and a reconciling column if they so wish, but this is not mandatory.

IFRS7B10A

16. If an outflow of cash could occur either significantly earlier than indicated or be for significantly different amounts from those indicated in the entity's disclosures about its exposure to liquidity risk, the entity should state that fact and provide quantitative information that enables users of its financial statements to evaluate the extent of this risk. This disclosure is not necessary if that information is included in the contractual maturity analysis.

Notes to the consolidated financial statements

(All amounts in C thousands unless otherwise stated)

Financing arrangements

IFRS7 p39(c)

17. Committed borrowing facilities are a major element of liquidity management. Entities should therefore consider providing information about their undrawn facilities. IAS 7, 'Statements of cash flows', also recommends disclosure of undrawn borrowing facilities that may be available for future operating activities and to settle capital commitments, indicating any restrictions on the use of these facilities.

Market risk

IFRS7 p40(a)(b)

18. Entities should disclose a sensitivity analysis for each type of market risk (currency, interest rate and other price risk) to which an entity is exposed at the end of the reporting period, showing how profit or loss and equity would have been affected by 'reasonably possible' changes in the relevant risk variable, as well as the methods and assumptions used in preparing such an analysis.

IFRS7 p40(c)

19. If there have been any changes in methods and assumptions from the previous period, this should be disclosed, together with the reasons for the change.

Foreign currency risk

IFRS7B23

20. Foreign currency risk can only arise on financial instruments that are denominated in a currency other than the functional currency in which they are measured. Translation related risks are therefore not included in the assessment of the entity's exposure to currency risks. Translation exposures arise from financial and non-financial items held by an entity (for example, a subsidiary) with a functional currency different from the group's presentation currency. However, foreign currency denominated inter– company receivables and payables that do not form part of a net investment in a foreign operation are included in the sensitivity analysis for foreign currency risks, because even though the balances eliminate in the consolidated balance sheet, the effect on profit or loss of their revaluation under IAS 21 is not fully eliminated.

Interest rate risk

21. Sensitivity to changes in interest rates is relevant to financial assets or financial liabilities bearing floating interest rates due to the risk that future cash flows will fluctuate. However, sensitivity will also be relevant to fixed rate financial assets and financial liabilities that are re-measured to fair value.

Fair value disclosures

Financial instruments carried at other than fair value

IFRS7p25, 29

22. An entity should disclose the fair value for each class of financial assets and financial liabilities (see paragraph 3 above) in a way that permits it to be compared with its carrying amount. Fair values do not need to be disclosed for the following:
(a) when the carrying amount is a reasonable approximation of fair value;
(b) investments in equity instruments (and derivatives linked to such equity instruments) that do not have a quoted market price in an active market and that are measured at cost in accordance with IAS 39 because their fair value cannot be measured reliably; and
(c) A contract containing a discretionary participation feature (as described in IFRS 4, 'Insurance contracts') where the fair value of that feature cannot be measured reliably.

(All amounts in C thousands unless otherwise stated)

23. The information about the fair values can be provided either in a combined financial instruments note or in the individual notes. However, fair values should be separately disclosed for each class of financial instrument (see paragraph 3 above), which means that each line item in the table would have to be broken down into individual classes. For that reason, IFRS GAAP plc has chosen to provide the information in the relevant notes.

Methods and assumptions in determining fair value

IFRS13p91

24. An entity shall disclose information that helps users of its financial statements assess both of the following:
(a) for assets and liabilities that are measured at fair value on a recurring or non-recurring basis in the statement of financial position after initial recognition, the valuation techniques and inputs used to develop those measurements.
(b) for recurring fair value measurements using significant unobservable inputs (Level 3), the effect of the measurements on profit or loss or other comprehensive income for the period.

Financial instruments measured at cost where fair value cannot be determined reliably

IFRS7p30

25. If the fair value of investments in unquoted equity instruments, derivatives linked to such equity instruments or a contract containing a discretionary participation feature (as described in IFRS 4, 'Insurance contracts') cannot be measured reliably, the entity should disclose:
(a) the fact that fair value information has not been disclosed because it cannot be measured reliably;
(b) a description of the financial instruments, their carrying amount and an explanation of why fair value cannot be measured reliably;
(c) information about the market for the instruments;
(d) information about whether and how the entity intends to dispose of the financial instruments; and
(e) if the instruments are subsequently derecognised, that fact, their carrying amount at the time of derecognition and the amount of gain or loss recognised.

Fair value measurements recognised in the balance sheet

IFRS13p93

26. For fair value measurements recognised in the balance sheet, the entity should also disclose for each class of financial instruments:
(a) the level in the fair value hierarchy into which the fair value measurements are categorised;
(b) any significant transfers between level 1 and level 2 of the fair value hierarchy and the reasons for those transfers;
(c) for fair value measurements in level 3 of the hierarchy, a reconciliation from the beginning balances to the ending balances, showing separately changes during the period attributable to the following:
(i) total gains or losses for the period recognised in profit or loss and the line item(s) which they are recognised, together with a description of where they are presented in the statement of comprehensive income or the income statement (as applicable);
(ii) total gains or losses recognised in other comprehensive income;
(iii) purchases, sales issues and settlements (each type disclosed separately); and
(iv) transfers into or out of level 3 and the reasons for those transfers;

(All amounts in C thousands unless otherwise stated)

(d) for recurring fair value measurements categorised within Level 3 of the fair value hierarchy, the amount of the total gains or losses for the period included in profit or loss that is attributable to the change in unrealised gains or losses relating to those assets and liabilities held at the end of the reporting period, and the line item(s) in profit or loss in which those unrealised gains or losses are recognised.

(e) for recurring fair value measurements in level 3:

    (i) for all such measurements, a narrative description of the sensitivity of the fair value measurement to changes in unobservable inputs if a change in those inputs to a different amount might result in a significantly higher or lower fair value measurement. If there are interrelationships between those inputs and other unobservable inputs used in the fair value measurement, an entity shall also provide a description of those interrelationships and of how they might magnify or mitigate the effect of changes in the unobservable inputs on the fair value measurement. To comply with that disclosure requirement, the narrative description of the sensitivity to changes in unobservable inputs shall include, at a minimum, the unobservable inputs disclosed.

    (ii) for financial assets and financial liabilities, if changing one or more of the unobservable inputs to reflect reasonably possible alternative assumptions would change fair value significantly, an entity shall state that fact and disclose the effect of those changes. The entity shall disclose how the effect of a change to reflect a reasonably possible alternative assumption was calculated. For that purpose, significance shall be judged with respect to profit or loss, and total assets or total liabilities, or, when changes in fair value are recognised in other comprehensive income, total equity.

IFRS13p93(b) 27. Entities should classify fair value measurements using a fair value hierarchy that reflects the significance of the inputs used in making the measurements. The fair value hierarchy should have the following levels:

(a) Level 1: quoted prices (unadjusted) in active markets for identical assets or liabilities.

(b) Level 2: inputs other than quoted prices that are observable for the asset or liability, either directly (for example, as prices) or indirectly (for example, derived from prices).

(c) Level 3: inputs for the asset or liability that are not based on observable market data.

The appropriate level is determined on the basis of the lowest level input that is significant to the fair value measurement.

Additional information where quantitative data about risk exposure is unrepresentative

IFRS7p35, p42 28. If the quantitative data disclosed under paragraphs 7, 9, 10 and 14 above is unrepresentative of the entity's exposure to risk during the period, the entity should provide further information that is representative. If the sensitivity analyses are unrepresentative of a risk inherent in a financial instrument (for example, where the year end exposure does not reflect the exposure during the year), the entity should disclose that fact and the reason why the sensitivity analyses are unrepresentative.

(All amounts in C thousands unless otherwise stated)

4 Critical accounting estimates and judgements

Estimates and judgements are continually evaluated and are based on historical experience and other factors, including expectations of future events that are believed to be reasonable under the circumstances.

1p125

4.1 Critical accounting estimates and assumptions

The group makes estimates and assumptions concerning the future. The resulting accounting estimates will, by definition, seldom equal the related actual results. The estimates and assumptions that have a significant risk of causing a material adjustment to the carrying amounts of assets and liabilities within the next financial year are addressed below.

(a) Estimated impairment of goodwill

The group tests annually whether goodwill has suffered any impairment, in accordance with the accounting policy stated in note 2.6. The recoverable amounts of cash-generating units have been determined based on value-in-use calculations. These calculations require the use of estimates (note 17).

1p129,
36p134(f)(i)-
(iii)

An impairment charge of C4,650 arose in the wholesale CGU in Step-land (included in the Russian operating segment) during the course of the 2013 year, resulting in the carrying amount of the CGU being written down to its recoverable amount. If the budgeted gross margin used in the value-in-use calculation for the wholesale CGU in Step-land had been 10% lower than management's estimates at 31 December 2013 (for example, 45.5% instead of 55.5%), the group would have recognised a further impairment of goodwill by C100 and would need to reduce the carrying value of property, plant and equipment by C300.

If the estimated cost of capital used in determining the pre-tax discount rate for the wholesale CGU in Step-land had been 1% higher than management's estimates (for example, 14.8% instead of 13.8%), the group would have recognised a further impairment against goodwill of C300.

(b) Income taxes

The group is subject to income taxes in numerous jurisdictions. Significant judgement is required in determining the worldwide provision for income taxes. There are many transactions and calculations for which the ultimate tax determination is uncertain. The group recognises liabilities for anticipated tax audit issues based on estimates of whether additional taxes will be due. Where the final tax outcome of these matters is different from the amounts that were initially recorded, such differences will impact the current and deferred income tax assets and liabilities in the period in which such determination is made.

Were the actual final outcome (on the judgement areas) of expected cash flows to differ by 10% from management's estimates, the group would need to:
- increase the income tax liability by C120 and the deferred tax liability by C230, if unfavourable; or
- decrease the income tax liability by C110 and the deferred tax liability by C215, if favourable.

(All amounts in C thousands unless otherwise stated)

(c) Fair value of derivatives and other financial instruments

IFRS13p91
The fair value of financial instruments that are not traded in an active market (for example, over-the-counter derivatives) is determined by using valuation techniques. The group uses its judgement to select a variety of methods and make assumptions that are mainly based on market conditions existing at the end of each reporting period. The group has used discounted cash flow analysis for various foreign exchange contracts that are not traded in active markets.

The carrying amount of foreign exchange contracts would be an estimated C12 lower or C15 higher were the discount rate used in the discount cash flow analysis to differ by 10% from management's estimates.

(d) Revenue recognition

The group uses the percentage-of-completion method in accounting for its fixed-price contracts to deliver design services. Use of the percentage-of-completion method requires the group to estimate the services performed to date as a proportion of the total services to be performed. Were the proportion of services performed to total services to be performed to differ by 10% from management's estimates, the amount of revenue recognised in the year would be increased by C1,175 if the proportion performed were increased, or would be decreased by C1,160 if the proportion performed were decreased.

(e) Pension benefits

The present value of the pension obligations depends on a number of factors that are determined on an actuarial basis using a number of assumptions. The assumptions used in determining the net cost (income) for pensions include the discount rate. Any changes in these assumptions will impact the carrying amount of pension obligations.

The group determines the appropriate discount rate at the end of each year. This is the interest rate that should be used to determine the present value of estimated future cash outflows expected to be required to settle the pension obligations. In determining the appropriate discount rate, the group considers the interest rates of high-quality corporate bonds that are denominated in the currency in which the benefits will be paid and that have terms to maturity approximating the terms of the related pension obligation.

Other key assumptions for pension obligations are based in part on current market conditions. Additional information is disclosed in note 33.

1p122
4.2 Critical judgements in applying the entity's accounting policies

(a) Revenue recognition

The group has recognised revenue amounting to C950 for sales of goods to L&Co in the UK during 2013. The buyer has the right to return the goods if their customers are dissatisfied. The group believes that, based on past experience with similar sales, the dissatisfaction rate will not exceed 3%. The group has, therefore, recognised revenue on this transaction with a corresponding provision against revenue for estimated returns. If the estimate changes by 1%, revenue will be reduced/increased by C10.

(All amounts in C thousands unless otherwise stated)

(b) Impairment of available-for-sale equity investments

The group follows the guidance of IAS 39 to determine when an available-for-sale equity investment is impaired. This determination requires significant judgement. In making this judgement, the group evaluates, among other factors, the duration and extent to which the fair value of an investment is less than its cost; and the financial health of and short-term business outlook for the investee, including factors such as industry and sector performance, changes in technology and operational and financing cash flow.

If all of the declines in fair value below cost were considered significant or prolonged, the group would suffer an additional loss of C1,300 in its 2013 financial statements, being the transfer of the accumulated fair value adjustments recognised in equity on the impaired available-for-sale financial assets to the income statement.

(c) Consolidation of entities in which the group holds less than 50%.

Management consider that the group has de facto control of Delta Inc even though it has less than 50% of the voting rights. The group is the majority shareholder of Delta Inc with a 40% equity interest, while all other shareholders individually own less than 1% of its equity shares. There is no history of other shareholders forming a group to exercise their votes collectively.

(d) Investment in Alpha Limited

Management has assessed the level of influence that the Group has on Alpha Limited and determined that it has significant influence even though the share holding is below 20% because of the board representation and contractual terms. Consequently, this investment has been classified as an associate.

(e) Joint arrangements

IFRS GAAP plc holds 50% of the voting rights of its joint arrangement. The group has joint control over this arrangement as under the contractual agreements, unanimous consent is required from all parties to the agreements for all relevant activities.

The group's joint arrangement is structured as a limited company and provides the group and the parties to the agreements with rights to the net assets of the limited company under the arrangements. Therefore, this arrangement is classified as a joint venture.

5 Segment information

IFRS8p22(a) The strategic steering committee is the group's chief operating decision-maker. Management has determined the operating segments based on the information reviewed by the strategic steering committee for the purposes of allocating resources and assessing performance.

IFRS8p22(a)(b) The strategic steering committee considers the business from both a geographic and product perspective. Geographically, management considers the performance in the UK, US, China, Russia and Europe. From a product perspective, management separately considers the wholesale and retail activities in these geographies. The group's retail activities are only in the UK and US. The wholesale segments derive their revenue primarily from the manufacture and wholesale sale of the group's own

Notes to the consolidated financial statements

(All amounts in C thousands unless otherwise stated)

brand of shoes, Footsy Tootsy. The UK and US retail segments derive their revenue from retail sales of shoe and leather goods including the group's own brand and other major retail shoe brands.

IFRS8p22(a) Although the China segment does not meet the quantitative thresholds required by IFRS 8 for reportable segments, management has concluded that this segment should be reported, as it is closely monitored by the strategic steering committee as a potential growth region and is expected to materially contribute to group revenue in the future.

IFRS8p18 During 2012, US retail did not qualify as a reportable operating segment. However, with the acquisition in 2013 of ABC Group (see note 39), retail qualifies as a reportable operating segment, the comparatives have been restated.

IFRS8p16 All other segments primarily relate to the sale of design services and goods transportation services to other shoe manufacturers in the UK and Europe and wholesale shoe revenue from the Central American region. These activities are excluded from the reportable operating segments, as these activities are not reviewed by the strategic steering committee.

IFRS8p28 The strategic steering committee assesses the performance of the operating segments based on a measure of adjusted EBITDA. This measurement basis excludes discontinued operations and the effects of non-recurring expenditure from the operating segments such as restructuring costs, legal expenses and goodwill impairments when the impairment is the result of an isolated, non-recurring event. The measure also excludes the effects of equity-settled share-based payments and unrealised gains/losses on financial instruments. Interest income and expenditure are not allocated to segments, as this type of activity is driven by the central treasury function, which manages the cash position of the group.

Revenue

IFRS8p27(a) Sales between segments are carried out at arm's length. The revenue from external parties reported to the strategic steering committee is measured in a manner consistent with that in the income statement.

	Year ended 31 December 2013			Year ended 31 December 2012 Restated		
	Total segment revenue	Inter-segment revenue	Revenue from external customers	Total segment revenue	Inter-segment revenue	Revenue from external customers
UK wholesale	46,638	(11,403)	**35,235**	42,284	(11,457)	30,827
UK retail	43,257	–	**43,257**	31,682	–	31,682
US wholesale	28,820	(7,364)	**21,456**	18,990	(6,798)	12,192
US retail	42,672	–	**42,672**	2,390	–	2,390
Russia wholesale	26,273	(5,255)	**21,018**	8,778	(1,756)	7,022
China wholesale	5,818	(1,164)	**4,654**	3,209	(642)	2,567
Europe wholesale	40,273	(8,055)	**32,218**	26,223	(5,245)	20,978
All other segments	13,155	(2,631)	**10,524**	5,724	(1,022)	4,702
Total	246,906	(35,872)	**211,034**	139,280	(26,920)	112,360

(All amounts in C thousands unless otherwise stated)

IFRS8p28(b)   **EBITDA**

	Year ended 31 December 2013	Year ended 31 December 2012 Restated
	Adjusted EBITDA	Adjusted EBITDA
UK wholesale	**17,298**	17,183
UK retail	**9,550**	800
US wholesale	**9,146**	10,369
US retail	**9,686**	1,298
Russia wholesale	**12,322**	3,471
China wholesale	**2,323**	1,506
Europe wholesale	**16,003**	10,755
All other segments	**3,504**	1,682
Total	**79,832**	47,064
Depreciation	**(17,754)**	(9,662)
Amortisation	**(800)**	(565)
Restructuring costs	**(1,986)**	–
Legal expenses	**(737)**	(855)
Goodwill impairment	**(4,650)**	–
Unrealised financial instrument gains	**102**	101
Share options granted to directors and employees	**(690)**	(822)
Finance costs – net	**(6,443)**	(10,588)
Other	**2,059**	1,037
Profit before tax and discontinued operations	**48,933**	25,710

(All amounts in C thousands unless otherwise stated)

IFRS8p23   **Other profit and loss disclosures[1]**

	Year ended 31 December 2013				
	Depreciation and amortisation	Goodwill impairment	Restructuring costs	Income tax expense	Share of profit from associates
UK wholesale	(3,226)	–	–	(2,550)	200
UK retail	(3,830)	–	–	(2,780)	–
US wholesale	(1,894)	–	–	(1,395)	–
US retail	(3,789)	–	–	(3,040)	–
Russia wholesale	(2,454)	(4,650)	(1,986)	(1,591)	–
China wholesale	(386)	–	–	(365)	–
Europe wholesale	(2,706)	–	–	(2,490)	–
All other segments	(269)	–	–	(400)	15
Total	**(18,554)**	**(4,650)**	**(1,986)**	**(14,611)**	**215**

	Year ended 31 December 2012 Restated				
	Depreciation and amortisation	Goodwill impairment	Restructuring costs	Income tax expense	Share of profit from associates
UK wholesale	(3,801)	–	–	(2,772)	155
UK retail	(201)	–	–	(650)	–
US wholesale	(2,448)	–	–	(1,407)	–
US retail	(199)	–	–	(489)	–
Russia wholesale	(453)	–	–	(509)	–
China wholesale	(286)	–	–	(150)	–
Europe wholesale	(2,701)	–	–	(2,201)	–
All other segments	(138)	–	–	(492)	(10)
Total	(10,227)	–	–	(8,670)	145

See note 17 for details of the impairment of goodwill of C4,650 in the Russian operating segment in 2013 relating to the decision to reduce manufacturing output. There has been no further impact on the measurement of the group's assets and liabilities. There was no impairment charge or restructuring costs recognised in 2012.

IFRS8p27(f)   Due to the European operations utilising excess capacity in certain Russian assets that are geographically close to the European region, a portion of the depreciation charge of C197 (2012: C50) relating to the Russian assets has been allocated to the European segment to take account of this.

---

[1] Paragraph 23 of IFRS 8 requires disclosures of interest revenue and expense even if not included in the measure of segment profit and loss. This disclosure has not been included in the illustrative because these balances are not allocated to the segments.

(All amounts in C thousands unless otherwise stated)

IFRS8p23,
IFRS8p24,
IFRS8p28(c)

Asset[1]

	Year ended 31 December 2013			Year ended 31 December 2012 Restated		
	Total assets	Invest- ments in associates and joint ventures	Additions to non-current assets[2]	Total assets	Invest- ments in associates and joint ventures	Additions to non-current assets[2]
UK wholesale	46,957	–	–	43,320	–	–
UK retail	46,197	–	35,543	9,580	–	47
US wholesale	27,313	–	–	32,967	–	–
US retail	45,529	–	39,817	8,550	–	46
Russia	22,659	–	–	5,067	–	–
China	6,226	–	11,380	20,899	–	2,971
Europe	47,912	18,649	1,222	40,259	17,053	2,543
All other segments	22,184	–	278	49,270	–	1,135
Total	**264,977**	**18,649**	**88,240**	209,912	17,053	6,742
Unallocated						
Deferred tax	3,546			3,383		
Available-for-sale financial assets	19,370			14,910		
Financial assets at fair value through profit and loss	11,820			7,972		
Derivative financial instruments	1,464			1,196		
Assets of disposal group classified as held for sale`	3,333					
Total assets per the balance sheet	**304,510**			237,373		

IFRS8p27(c)   The amounts provided to the strategic steering committee with respect to total assets are measured in a manner consistent with that of the financial statements. These assets are allocated based on the operations of the segment and the physical location of the asset.

Investment in shares (classified as available-for-sale financial assets or financial assets at fair value through profit or loss) held by the group are not considered to be segment assets but rather are managed by the treasury function. The measure of assets reviewed by the CODM does not include assets held for sale. The group's interest-bearing liabilities are not considered to be segment liabilities but rather are managed by the treasury function.

---

[1] The measure of assets has been disclosed for each reportable segment as is regularly provided to the chief operating decision-maker. If the chief operating decision-maker reviews a measure of liabilities, this should also be disclosed.

[2] Additions to non-current assets excludes other than financial instruments and deferred tax assets.

Notes to the consolidated financial statements

(All amounts in C thousands unless otherwise stated)

Entity-wide information

IFRS8p32   Breakdown of the revenue from all services is as follows:

	2013	2012 Restated
Analysis of revenue by category:		
– Sales of goods	**202,884**	104,495
– Revenue from services	**8,000**	7,800
– Royalty income	**150**	65
Total	**211,034**	112,360

IFRS8p33(a)   The group is domiciled in the UK. The result of its revenue from external customers in the UK is C50,697 (2012: C48,951), and the total of revenue from external customers from other countries is C160,337 (2012: C63,409). The breakdown of the major component of the total of revenue from external customers from other countries is disclosed above.

IFRS8p33(b)   The total of non-current assets other than financial instruments and deferred tax assets (there are no employment benefit assets and rights arising under insurance contracts) located in the UK is C49,696 (2012: C39,567), and the total of such non-current assets located in other countries is C146,762 (2012: C93,299).

IFRS8p34   Revenues of approximately C32,023 (2012: C28,034) are derived from a single external customer. These revenues are attributable to the US retail and UK wholesale segments.

6 Exceptional items

Items that are material either because of their size or their nature, or that are non-recurring are considered as exceptional items and are presented within the line items to which they best relate. During the year, the exceptional items as detailed below have been included in cost of sales in the income statement.

An analysis of the amount presented as exceptional item in these financial statements is given below.

	2013	2012
Operating items:		
– Inventory write-down	**3,117**	–

The inventory write-down of C3,117 relates to leather accessories that have been destroyed by fire in an accident. This amount is included within cost of sales in the income statement.

(All amounts in C thousands unless otherwise stated)

7 Other income

		2013	2012
	Gain on re-measuring to fair value the existing interest in ABC Group on acquisition of control (note 39)	**850**	–
18p35(b)(v)	Dividend income on available-for-sale financial assets	**1,100**	883
18p35(b)(v)	Dividend income on financial assets at fair value through profit or loss	**800**	310
	Investment income	**2,750**	1,193
	Insurance reimbursement	–	66
	Total	**2,750**	1,259

The insurance reimbursement relates to the excess of insurance proceeds over the carrying values of goods damaged.

8 Other (losses)/gains – net

IFRS7p20(a)(i)		2013	2012
	Financial assets at fair value through profit or loss (note 23):		
	– Fair value losses	**(508)**	(238)
	– Fair value gains	**593**	–
IFRS7p20(a)(i)	Foreign exchange forward contracts:		
	– Held for trading	**86**	88
21p52(a)	– Net foreign exchange (losses)/gains (note15)	**(277)**	200
IFRS7p24(a)	Ineffectiveness on fair value hedges (note 20)	**(1)**	(1)
IFRS7p24(b)	Ineffectiveness on cash flow hedges (note 20)	**17**	14
	Total	**(90)**	63

9 Expenses by nature

		2013	2012 Restated
1p104	Changes in inventories of finished goods and work in progress	**6,950**	(2,300)
1p104	Raw material and consumables used	**53,302**	31,845
1p104	Employee benefit expense (note 10)	**40,310**	15,577
1p104	Depreciation, amortisation and impairment charges (notes 16 and 17)	**23,204**	10,227
1p104	Transportation expenses	**8,584**	6,236
1p104	Advertising costs	**14,265**	6,662
1p104	Operating lease payments (note 16)	**10,604**	8,500
1p104	Other expenses	**2,781**	1,659
	Total cost of sales, distribution costs and administrative expenses	**160,000**	78,406

Notes to the consolidated financial statements

(All amounts in C thousands unless otherwise stated)

10 Employee benefit expense

		2013	2012 Restated
19Rp171	Wages and salaries, including restructuring costs C799 (2012: nil) and other termination benefits C1,600 (2012: nil) (note 35 and note 41)	28,363	10,041
	Social security costs	9,369	3,802
IFRS2p51(a)	Share options granted to directors and employees (notes 27 and 28)	690	822
19Rp53	Pension costs – defined contribution plans	756	232
19Rp141	Pension costs – defined benefit plans (note 33)	948	561
19Rp141	Other post-employment benefits (note 33)	184	119
		40,310	**15,577**

11 Finance income and costs

		2013	2012 Restated
IFRS7p20(b)	Interest expense:		
	– Bank borrowings	(5,317)	(10,646)
	– Dividend on redeemable preference shares (note 31)	(1,950)	(1,950)
	– Convertible bond (note 31)	(3,083)	–
	– Finance lease liabilities	(547)	(646)
37p84(e)	– Provisions: unwinding of discount (note 21 and 35)	(47)	(39)
21p52(a)	Net foreign exchange gains on financing activities (note 15)	2,594	996
	Fair value gains on financial instruments:		
IFRS7p23(d)	– Interest rate swaps: cash flow hedges, transfer from equity	102	88
IFRS7p24(a)(i)	– Interest rate swaps: fair value hedges	16	31
	Fair value adjustment of bank borrowings attributable to		
IFRS7p24(a)(ii)	interest rate risk	(16)	(31)
	Total finance costs	(8,248)	(12,197)
	Less: amounts capitalised on qualifying assets	75	–
	Finance costs	**(8,173)**	**(12,197)**
	Finance income:		
	– Interest income on short-term bank deposits	550	489
IFRS7p20(b)	– Interest income on available-for-sale financial assets	963	984
IFRS7p20(b)	– Interest income on loans to related parties (note 41)	217	136
	Finance income	**1,730**	**1,609**
	Net finance costs	**(6,443)**	**(10,588)**

(All amounts in C thousands unless otherwise stated)

12 Investments accounted for using the equity method

The amounts recognised in the balance sheet are as follows:

	2013	2012 Restated
Associates	13,373	13,244
Joint ventures	5,276	3,809
At 31 December	**18,649**	17,053

The amounts recognised in the income statement are as follows:

	2013	2012 Restated
Associates	215	145
Joint ventures	1,467	877
At 31 December	**1,682**	1,022

12(a) Investment in associates

IFRS 12p21(a) Set out below are the associates of the group as at 31 December 2013, which, in the opinion of the directors, are material to the group. The associates as listed below have share capital consisting solely of ordinary shares, which are held directly by the group; the country of incorporation or registration is also their principal place of business.

Nature of investment in associates 2013 and 2012:

Name of entity	Place of business/ country of incorporation	% of ownership interest	Nature of the relationship	Measurement method
Alpha Limited	Cyprus	18	Note 1	Equity
Beta SA	Greece	30	Note 2	Equity

Note 1: Alpha Limited provides products and services to the footware industry. Alpha is a strategic partnership for the group, providing access to new customers and markets in Europe.

Note 2: Beta SA manufactures parts for the footware industry and distributes its products globally. Beta SA is strategic for the group's growth in the European market and provides the group with access to expertise in efficient manufacturing processes for its footware business and access to key fashion trends.

IFRS 12p21(b)(iii) As at 31 December 2013, the fair value of the groups interest in Beta SA, which is listed on the Euro Money Stock Exchange, was C13,513 (2012: C12,873) and the carrying amount of the group's interest was C11,997 (2012: C11,240).

Alpha Limited is a private company and there is no quoted market price available for its shares.

IFRS12p23(b) There are no contingent liabilities relating to the group's interest in the associates

Notes to the consolidated financial statements

(All amounts in C thousands unless otherwise stated)

Summarised financial information for associates

Set out below are the summarised financial information for Alpha Limited and Beta SA which are accounted for using the equity method.

Summarised balance sheet

		Alpha Limited		Beta SA		Total	
		As at 31 December		As at 31 December		As at 31 December	
		2013	2012	**2013**	2012	**2013**	2012
	Current						
IFRS12pB13(a)	Cash and cash equivalents	**1,170**	804	**5,171**	8,296	**6,341**	9,100
IFRS12p B12(b)(i)	Other current assets (excluding cash)	**2,433**	2,635	**7,981**	9,722	**10,414**	12,357
IFRS12p B12(b)(i)	Total current assets	**3,603**	3,439	**13,152**	18,018	**16,755**	21,457
IFRS12pB13(b)	Financial liabiliites (excluding trade payables)	**(808)**	(558)	**(8,375)**	(8,050)	**(9,183)**	(8,608)
IFRS12p B12(b)(iii)	Other current liabilities (including trade payables)	**(2,817)**	(2,635)	**(6,017)**	(14,255)	**(8,834)**	(16,890)
IFRS12p B12(b)(iii)	Total current liabilities	**(3,625)**	(3,193)	**(14,392)**	(22,305)	**(18,017)**	(25,498)
IFRS12p B12(b)(ii)	**Non-current** Assets	**13,340**	14,751	**53,201**	54,143	**66,541**	68,894
IFRS12p B13(c)	Financial liabilities	**(4,941)**	(3,647)	**(9,689)**	(8,040)	**(14,630)**	(11,687)
IFRS12p B12(b)(iv)	Other liabilities	**(733)**	(217)	**(2,282)**	(4,349)	**(3,015)**	(4,566)
	Total non-current liabiliites	**(5,674)**	(3,864)	**(11,971)**	(12,389)	**(17,645)**	(16,253)
DV	**Net assets**	**7,644**	11,133	**39,990**	37,467	**47,634**	48,600

(All amounts in C thousands unless otherwise stated)

Summarised statement of comprehensive income

		Alpha Limited		Beta SA		Total	
		For period ended 31 December		For period ended 31 December		For period ended 31 December	
		2013	2012	**2013**	2012	**2013**	2012
IFRS12p B12(b)(v)	Revenue	**11,023**	15,012	**26,158**	23,880	**37,181**	38,892
IFRS12p B13(d)	Depreciation and amortisation	**(2,576)**	(1,864)	**(3,950)**	(3,376)	**(6,526)**	(5,240)
IFRS12p B13(e)	Interest income[1]	**–**	–	**–**	–	**–**	–
IFRS12p B13(e)(f)	Interest expense	**(1,075)**	(735)	**(1,094)**	(1,303)	**(2,169)**	(2,038)
IFRS12p B12(b)(vi)	**Profit or loss from continuing operations**	**(3,531)**	(2,230)	**3,443**	2,109	**(88)**	(121)
IFRS12p B13(g)	Income tax expense	**175**	208	**(713)**	(412)	**(538)**	(204)
IFRS12p B12(b)(vi)	**Post-tax profit from continuing operations**	**(3,356)**	(2,022)	**2,730**	1,697	**(626)**	(325)
IFRS12p B12(b)(vii)	**Post-tax profit from discontinued operations**[1]	**–**	–	**–**	–	**–**	–
IFRS12p B12(b)(viii)	**Other comprehensive income**	**–**	–	**(40)**	(47)	**(40)**	(47)
IFRS12p B12(b)(ix)	**Total comprehensive income**	**(3,356)**	(2,022)	**2,690**	1,650	**(666)**	(372)
IFRS12pb12(a)	**Dividends received from associate**[1]	**–**	–	**–**	–	**–**	–

IFRS12pB14   The information above reflects the amounts presented in the financial statements of the associates (and not IFRS GAAP plc's share of those amounts) adjusted for differences in accounting policies between the group and the associates.

Commentary – summarised financial information

Summarised financial information is required for the group's interest in material associates; however, IFRS GAAP plc has provided the total amounts voluntarily.

[1] Some of the line items above have a nil balance but have still been included for illustrative purposes only.

Notes to the consolidated financial statements

(All amounts in C thousands unless otherwise stated)

Reconciliation of summarised financial information

IFRS12 pB14(b) Reconciliation of the summarised financial information presented to the carrying amount of its interest in associates

Summarised financial information	Alpha Limited		Beta SA		Total	
	2013	2012	**2013**	2012	**2013**	2012
Opening net assets 1 January	**11,133**	12,977	**37,467**	35,573	**48,600**	48,550
Profit/(loss) for the period	(3,356)	(2,022)	2,730	1,697	(626)	(325)
Other comprehensive income	–	–	(40)	(47)	(40)	(47)
Foreign exchange differences	(133)	178	(167)	243	(300)	421
Closing net assets	**7,644**	11,133	**39,990**	37,466	**47,634**	48,599
Interest in associates (18%; 30%)	1,376	2,004	11,997	11,240	13,373	13,244
Goodwill[1]	–	–	–	–	–	–
Carrying value	**1,376**	2,004	**11,997**	11,240	**13,373**	13,244

12(b) Investment in joint venture

	2013	2012
At 1 January	**3,809**	2,932
Share of profit	**1,467**	877
Other comprehensive income[1]	–	–
At 31 December	**5,276**	3,809

IFRS 12p21(a) The joint venture listed below has share capital consisting solely of ordinary shares, which is held directly by the group.

Nature of investment in joint ventures 2013 and 2012

Name of entity	Place of business/country of incorporation	% of ownership interest	Nature of the relationship	Measurement method
Gamma Ltd	United Kingdom	50	Note 1	Equity

Note 1: Gamma Ltd provides products and services to the footware industry in the UK. Gamma Ltd is a strategic partnership for the group, providing access to new technology and processes for its footware business.

IFRS 12p21(b)(iii) Gamma Ltd is a private company and there is no quoted market price available for its shares.

[1] Some of the line items above have a nil balance but have still been included for illustrative purposes only.

(All amounts in C thousands unless otherwise stated)

Commentary – fair value of interest in joint venture

Where there is a quoted market price for an entity's investment in a joint venture, the fair value of that interest should be disclosed.

Commitments and contingent liabilities in respect of joint ventures

IFRS12p23(a) The group has the following commitments relating to its joint ventures.

	2013	2012
Commitment to provide funding if called	100	100

IFRS12p23(b) There are no contingent liabilities relating to the group's interest in the joint venture. Gamma Ltd has a contingent liability relating to an unresolved legal case relating to a contract dispute with a customer. As the case is at an early stage in proceedings it is not possible to determine the likelihood or amount of any settlement should Gamma Ltd not be successful.

Summarised financial information for joint ventures

IFRS12p 21(b)(ii) Set out below are the summarised financial information for Gamma Ltd which is accounted for using the equity method.

Summarised balance sheet

	As at 31 December 2013	2012
Current		
IFRS12pB13(a) Cash and cash equivalents	1,180	780
IFRS12p B12(b)(i) Other current assets (excluding cash)	7,368	4,776
IFRS12p B12(b)(i) Total current assets	8,548	5,556
IFRS12p B13(b) Financial liabiliites (excluding trade payables)	(1,104)	(1,094)
IFRS12p B12(b)(iii) Other current liabilities (including trade payables)	(890)	(726)
IFRS12p B12(b)(iii) Total current liabilities	(1,994)	(1,820)
Non-current		
IFRS12p B12(b)(ii) Assets	11,016	9,786
IFRS12p B13(c) Financial liabilities	(6,442)	(5,508)
IFRS12p B12(b)(iv) Other liabilities	(576)	(396)
Total non-current liabilities	(7,018)	(5,904)
DV **Net assets**	10,552	7,618

Notes to the consolidated financial statements

(All amounts in C thousands unless otherwise stated)

	Summarised statement of comprehensive income	For period ended 31 December	
		2013	**2012**
IFRS12p B12(b)(v)	Revenue	**23,620**	23,158
IFRS12pB13(d)	Depreciation and amortisation		
IFRS12pB13(e)	Interest income	**206**	648
IFRS12p B13(f)	Interest expense	**(1,760)**	(2,302)
IFRS12p B12(b)(vi)	**Profit or loss from continuing operations**	**5,750**	5,206
IFRS12p B13(g)	Income tax expense	**(2,816)**	(3,452)
IFRS12p B12(b)(vi)	**Post-tax profit from continuing operations**	**2,934**	1,754
IFRS12p B12(b)(vii)	**Post-tax profit from discontinued operations[1]**	**–**	–
IFRS12p B12(b)(viii)	**Other comprehensive income[1]**	**–**	–
IFRS12p B12(b)(ix)	**Total comprehensive income**	**2,934**	1,754
IFRS12pb12(a)	**Dividends received from joint venture or associate[1]**	**–**	–

IFRS12pB14 The information above reflects the amounts presented in the financial statements of the joint venture adjusted for differences in accounting policies between the group and the joint venture (and not IFRS GAAP plc's share of those amounts).

Reconciliation of summarised financial information

IFRS12 pB14(b) Reconciliation of the summarised financial information presented to the carrying amount of its interest in the joint venture.

Summarised financial information	2013	2012
Opening net assets 1 January	**7,618**	**5,864**
Profit/(loss) for the period	2,934	1,754
Other comprehensive income[1]	–	–
Closing net assets	**10,552**	**7,618**
Interest in joint venture @50%	5,276	3,809
Goodwill[1]	–	–
Carrying value	**5,276**	**3,809**

[1] Some of the line items above have a nil balance but have still been included for illustrative purposes only.

(All amounts in C thousands unless otherwise stated)

12(c) Principal subsidiaries

The group had the following subsidiaries at 31 December 2013

IFRS12p10(a),
12(a-c)   **Group and Company**

Name	Country of incorporation and place of business	Nature of business	Proportion of ordinary shares directly held by parent (%)	Proportion of ordinary shares held by the group (%)	Proportion of ordinary shares held by non-controlling interests (%)	Proportion of preference shares held by the group (%)
Treasury Limited	UK	Head office financing company	100	100	–	–
A Limited	UK	Intermediate holding company	–	100	–	100
O Limited	UK	Shoe manufacturer and wholesaler	–	85	15	–
Shoe Limited	UK	Shoe and leather goods retailer	–	100	–	–
L Limited	UK	Logistics company	100	100	–	–
D Limited	UK	Design services	100	100	–	–
Delta Inc	US	Shoe and leather goods retailer	–	40	60	–
ABC Group	US	Shoe and leather goods retailer	72	72	28	–
M GbmH	Germany	Shoe manufacturer and wholesaler	–	100	–	–
L SARL	France	Logistics company	–	100	–	–
E GbmH	Germany	Design services	–	100	–	–
C Group	China	Shoe manufacturer and wholesaler	–	100	–	–
R Group	Russia	Shoe manufacturer and wholesaler	–	100	–	–

All subsidiary undertakings are included in the consolidation. The proportion of the voting rights in the subsidiary undertakings held directly by the parent company do not differ from the proportion of ordinary shares held. The parent company further

(All amounts in C thousands unless otherwise stated)

does not have any shareholdings in the preference shares of subsidiary undertakings included in the group.

IFRS12 p12 (f) The total non-controlling interest for the period is C7,888, of which C5,327 is for ABC Group and C2,466 is attributed to Delta Inc. The non-controlling interest in respect of O Limited is not material.

Significant restrictions

IFRS12p 10(b)(i) Cash and short-term deposits of C1,394 are held in China and are subject to local exchange control regulations. These local exchange control regulations provide for restrictions on exporting capital from the country, other than through normal dividends.

Summarised financial information on subsidiaries with material non-controlling interests

IFRS12p12(g), B10(b) Set out below are the summarised financial information for each subsidiary that has non-controlling interests that are material to the group.

See note 40 for transactions with non-controlling interests.

Summarised balance sheet

	Delta Inc		ABC Group	
	As at 31 December		As at 31 December	
	2013	2012	2013	2012
Current				
Assets	5,890	4,828	16,935	14,742
Liabilities	(3,009)	(2,457)	(4,514)	(3,686)
Total current net assets	2,881	2,371	12,421	11,056
Non-current				
Assets	3,672	2,357	10,008	8,536
Liabilities	(2,565)	(1,161)	(3,848)	(1,742)
Total non-current net assets	1,107	1,196	6,160	6,794
Net assets	3,988	3,567	18,581	17,850

(All amounts in C thousands unless otherwise stated)

Summarised income statement

	Delta Inc		ABC Group	
	For period ended 31 December		**For period ended 31 December**	
	2013	2012	**2013**	2012
Revenue	**19,602**	17,883	**29,403**	26,825
Profit before income tax	**4,218**	3,007	**6,327**	6,611
Income tax expense/income	**(1,692)**	(1,411)	**(2,838)**	(2,667)
Post-tax profit from continuing operations	**2,526**	1,596	**3,489**	3,944
Post-tax profit from discontinued operations	**–**	–	**23**	19
Other comprehensive income	**369**	(203)	**554**	495
Total comprehensive income	**2,895**	1,393	**4,066**	4,458
Total comprehensive income allocated to non-controlling interests	**1,737**	836	**1,138**	–
Dividends paid to non-controlling interests	**1,770**	550	**150**	–

Summarised cash flows

	Delta Inc	ABC Group
	31 December 2013	**31 December 2013**
Cash flows from operating activities		
Cash generated from operations	6,854	6,586
Interest paid	(134)	(86)
Income tax paid	(1,534)	(2,748)
Net cash generated from operating activities	**5,186**	**3,752**
Net cash used in investing activities	**(1,218)**	**(1,225)**
Net cash used in financing activities	**(3,502)**	**(478)**
Net (decrease)/increase in cash and cash equivalents	**466**	**2,049**
Cash, cash equivalents and bank overdrafts at beginning of year	576	1,576
Exchange gains/(losses) on cash and cash equivalents	(56)	38
Cash and cash equivalents at end of year	**986**	**3,663**

IFRS12pB11   The information above is the amount before inter-company eliminations.

Notes to the consolidated financial statements

(All amounts in C thousands unless otherwise stated)

13 Income tax expense

	2013	2012 Restated
Current tax:		
12p80(a) Current tax on profits for the year	14,082	6,035
12p80(b) Adjustments in respect of prior years	150	–
Total current tax	14,232	6,035
Deferred tax (note 32):		
12p80(c) Origination and reversal of temporary differences	476	2,635
12p80(d) Impact of change in the Euravian tax rate[1]	(97)	–
Total deferred tax	379	2,635
Income tax expense	14,611	8,670

12p81(c) The tax on the group's profit before tax differs from the theoretical amount that would arise using the weighted average tax rate applicable to profits of the consolidated entities as follows:

	2013	2012 Restated
Profit before tax	48,933	25,710
Tax calculated at domestic tax rates applicable to profits in the respective countries	16,148	7,713
Tax effects of:		
– Associates results reported net of tax	57	(44)
– Income not subject to tax	(1,072)	(212)
– Expenses not deductible for tax purposes	845	866
– Utilisation of previously unrecognised tax losses	(1,450)	–
– Tax losses for which no deferred income tax asset was recognised	30	347
Re-measurement of deferred tax – change in Euravian tax rate	(97)	–
Adjustment in respect of prior years	150	–
Tax charge	14,611	8,670

12p81(d) The weighted average applicable tax rate was 33% (2012: 30%). The increase is caused by a change in the profitability of the group's subsidiaries in the respective countries partially offset by the impact of the reduction in the Euravian tax rate (see below).

12p81(d) During the year, as a result of the change in the Euravian corporation tax rate from 30% to 28% that was substantively enacted on 26 June 2013 and that will be effective from 1 April 2014, the relevant deferred tax balances have been re-measured. Deferred tax expected to reverse in the year to 31 December 2013 has been measured using the effective rate that will apply in Euravia for the period (28.5%).[2]

[1] The impact of change in Euravian tax rate is shown for illustrative purposes.
[2] If the effect of the proposed changes is material, disclosure should be given of the effect of the changes, either as disclosure of events after the reporting period or as future material adjustment to the carrying amounts of assets and liabilities. This disclosure does not need to be tailored or reconciled to the income statement.

(All amounts in C thousands unless otherwise stated)

1p125,10p21   Further reductions to the Euravian tax rate have been announced. The changes, which are expected to be enacted separately each year, propose to reduce the rate by 1% per annum to 24% by 1 April 2018. The changes had not been substantively enacted at the balance sheet date and, therefore, are not recognised in these financial statements.[1]

12p81(ab)   The tax (charge)/credit relating to components of other comprehensive income is as follows:

	2013		
		Tax (charge)	
	Before tax	/credit	After tax
Fair value gains:			
1p90 – Land and buildings	1,005	(250)	755
1p90 – Available-for-sale financial assets	560	(198)	362
1p90 Share of other comprehensive income of associates	(86)	–	(86)
1p90 Remeasurements of post employment benefit liabilities	119	(36)	83
1p90 Impact of change in the Euravian tax rate on deferred tax[2]	–	(10)	(10)
1p90 Cash flow hedges	97	(33)	64
1p90 Net investment hedge	(45)	–	(45)
1p90 Currency translation differences	2,401	–	2,401
IFRS3p59 Reclassification of revaluation of previously held interest in ABC Group	(850)	–	(850)
Other comprehensive income	**3,201**	**(527)**	**2,674**
Current tax[3]		–	
Deferred tax (note 32)		(527)	
		(527)	

[1] Disclosure in respect of the impact of change in Euravian tax rate is shown for illustrative purposes. UK companies will need to consider the impact of any tax rate changes which have been announced but not substantively enacted at the balance sheet date.
[2] The impact of change in Euravian tax rate is shown for illustrative purposes.
[3] There are no current tax items relating to other comprehensive income in these financial statements, but the line item is shown for illustrative purposes.

Notes to the consolidated financial statements

(All amounts in C thousands unless otherwise stated)

		2012 Restated		
			Tax (charge)	
		Before tax	/credit	After tax
	Fair value gains:			
1p90	– Land and buildings	1,133	(374)	759
1p90	– Available-for-sale financial assets	973	(61)	912
1p90	Share of other comprehensive income of associates	91	–	91
1p90	Remeasurements of post employment benefit liabilities	(910)	273	(637)
1p90	Impact of change in the Euravian tax rate on deferred tax[1]	–	–	–
1p90	Cash flow hedges	(3)	–	(3)
1p90	Net investment hedge	40	–	40
1p90	Currency translation differences	(922)	–	(922)
IFRS3p59	Reclassification of revaluation of previously held interest in ABC Group	–	–	–
	Other comprehensive income	402	(162)	240
	Current tax[2]		–	
	Deferred tax (note 32)		(162)	
			(162)	

12p81(a)   The income tax (charged)/credited directly to equity during the year is as follows:

	2013	2012
Current tax[3]		
Share option scheme	–	–
Deferred tax		
Share option scheme	**30**	20
Convertible bond – equity component[4] (note 29)	**(2,328)**	–
	(2,298)	20

In addition, deferred income tax of C49 (2012: C43) was transferred from other reserves (note 29) to retained earnings (note 28). This represents deferred tax on the difference between the actual depreciation on buildings and the equivalent depreciation based on the historical cost of buildings.

[1] The impact of change in Euravian tax rate is shown for illustrative purposes.
[2] There are no current tax items relating to other comprehensive income in these financial statements, but the line item is shown for illustrative purposes.
[3] IAS 12 requires disclosure of current tax charged/credited directly to equity, in addition to deferred tax. There are no current tax items shown directly in equity in these financial statements, but the line item is shown for illustrative purposes.
[4] It is assumed that the tax base on the convertible bond is not split between the debt and equity elements. If the tax base were split, this would impact the deferred tax position.

(All amounts in C thousands unless otherwise stated)

14 Earnings per share

(a) Basic

Basic earnings per share is calculated by dividing the profit attributable to equity holders of the company by the weighted average number of ordinary shares in issue during the year excluding ordinary shares purchased by the company and held as treasury shares (note 26).

		2013	2012 Restated
33p70(a)	Profit from continuing operations attributable to owners of the parent	31,774	16,184
	Profit from discontinued operations attributable to owners of the parent	100	120
	Total	**31,874**	16,304
33p70(b)	Weighted average number of ordinary shares in issue (thousands)	23,454	20,500

(b) Diluted

Diluted earnings per share is calculated by adjusting the weighted average number of ordinary shares outstanding to assume conversion of all dilutive potential ordinary shares. The company has two categories of dilutive potential ordinary shares: convertible debt and share options. The convertible debt is assumed to have been converted into ordinary shares, and the net profit is adjusted to eliminate the interest expense less the tax effect. For the share options, a calculation is done to determine the number of shares that could have been acquired at fair value (determined as the average annual market share price of the company's shares) based on the monetary value of the subscription rights attached to outstanding share options. The number of shares calculated as above is compared with the number of shares that would have been issued assuming the exercise of the share options.

		2013	2012 Restated
	Earnings		
	Profit from continuing operations attributable to owners of the parent	31,774	16,184
	Interest expense on convertible debt (net of tax)	2,158	–
33p70(a)	Profit used to determine diluted earnings per share	33,932	16,184
	Profit from discontinued operations attributable to owners of the parent	100	120
		34,032	16,304
	Weighted average number of ordinary shares in issue (thousands)	23,454	20,500
	Adjustment for:		
	– Assumed conversion of convertible debt (thousands)	3,300	–
	– Share options (thousands)	1,213	1,329
33p70(b)	Weighted average number of ordinary shares for diluted earnings per share (thousands)	27,967	21,829

Notes to the consolidated financial statements

(All amounts in C thousands unless otherwise stated)

15 Net foreign exchange gains/(losses)

21p52(a)   The exchange differences charged/credited to the income statement are included as follows:

	2013	2012 Restated
Other (losses)/gains – net (note 8)	(277)	200
Net finance costs (note 11)	2,594	996
Total	**2,317**	**1,196**

16 Property, plant and equipment

		Land and buildings	Vehicles and machinery	Furniture, fittings and equipment	Construc- tion in progress	Total
16p73(d)	**At 1 January 2012 (Restated)**					
	Cost or valuation	39,664	71,072	20,025	–	130,761
	Accumulated depreciation	(2,333)	(17,524)	(3,690)	–	(23,547)
	Net book amount	**37,331**	**53,548**	**16,335**	**–**	**107,214**
16p73(e)	**Year ended 31 December 2012 (Restated)**					
	Opening net book amount	37,331	53,548	16,335	–	107,214
16p73(e)(viii)	Exchange differences	(381)	(703)	(423)	–	(1,507)
16p73(e)(iv)	Revaluation surplus (note 29)	1,133	–	–	–	1,133
16p73(e)(i)	Additions	1,588	2,970	1,484	–	6,042
16p73(e)(ix)	Disposals (note 36)	–	(2,607)	(380)	–	(2,987)
16p73(e)(vii)	Depreciation charge (note 9)	(636)	(4,186)	(4,840)	–	(9,662)
	Closing net book amount	**39,035**	**49,022**	**12,176**	**–**	**100,233**
16p73(d)	**At 31 December 2012 (Restated)**					
	Cost or valuation	42,004	70,732	20,706	–	133,442
	Accumulated depreciation	(2,969)	(21,710)	(8,530)	–	(33,209)
	Net book amount	**39,035**	**49,022**	**12,176**	**–**	**100,233**
	Year ended 31 December 2013					
16p73(e)	Opening net book amount	39,035	49,022	12,176	–	100,233
16p73(e)(viii)	Exchange differences	846	1,280	342	–	2,468
16p73(e)(iv)	Revaluation surplus (note 29)	1,005	–	–	–	1,005
16p73(e)(iii)	Acquisition of subsidiary (note 39)	49,072	5,513	13,199	–	67,784
16p73(e)(i)	Additions	4,421	427	2,202	2,455	9,505
16p73(e)(ix)	Disposals (note 36)	(2,000)	(3,729)	(608)	–	(6,337)
	Transfers	1,245	–	–	(1,245)	–
16p73(e)(vii)	Depreciation charge (note 9)	(3,545)	(4,768)	(9,441)	–	(17,754)
IFRS5p38	Transferred to disposal group classified as held for sale	(341)	(1,222)	–	–	(1,563)
	Closing net book amount	**89,738**	**46,523**	**17,870**	**1,210**	**155,341**
16p73(d)	**At 31 December 2013**					
	Cost or valuation	96,593	74,223	35,841	1,210	207,867
	Accumulated depreciation	(6,855)	(27,700)	(17,971)	–	(52,526)
	Net book amount	**89,738**	**46,523**	**17,870**	**1,210**	**155,341**

(1p78(a))

(All amounts in C thousands unless otherwise stated)

DV	Property, plant and equipment transferred to the disposal group classified as held-for-sale amounts to C1,563 and relates to assets that are used by Shoes Limited (part of the UK wholesale segment). See note 25 for further details regarding the disposal group held for sale.
DV, 1p104	Depreciation expense of C8,054 (2012: C5,252) has been charged in 'cost of sales', C5,568 (2012: C2,410) in 'distribution costs' and C4,132 (2012: C2,000) in 'administrative expenses'.
17p35(c)	Lease rentals amounting to C1,172 (2012: C895) and C9,432 (2012: C7,605) relating to the lease of machinery and property, respectively, are included in the income statement (note 9).
	Construction work in progress as at 31 December, 2013 mainly comprises new shoe manufacturing equipment being constructed in the UK.
23p26	During the year, the group has capitalised borrowing costs amounting to C75 (2012: nil) on qualifying assets. Borrowing costs were capitalised at the weighted average rate of its general borrowings of 7.5%.
16p77(e)	If land and buildings were stated on the historical cost basis, the amounts would be as follows:

	2013	2012
Cost	**93,079**	37,684
Accumulated depreciation	**(6,131)**	(2,197)
Net book amount	**86,948**	35,487

16p74(a)	Bank borrowings are secured on land and buildings for the value of C37,680 (2012: C51,306) (note 31).
17p31(a)	Vehicles and machinery includes the following amounts where the group is a lessee under a finance lease:

	2013	2012
Cost-capitalised finance lease	**13,996**	14,074
Accumulated depreciation	**(5,150)**	(3,926)
Net book amount	**8,846**	10,148

17p31(e)	The group leases various vehicles and machinery under non-cancellable finance lease agreements. The lease terms are between 3 and 15 years, and ownership of the assets lies within the group.

Fair values of land and buildings

16p77(a)-(b)	An independent valuation of the group's land and buildings was performed by valuers to determine the fair value of the land and buildings as at 31 December 2013 and 2012. The revaluation surplus net of applicable deferred income taxes was credited to other comprehensive income and is shown in 'other reserves' in shareholders equity (note 29). The following table analyses the non-financial assets carried at fair value, by valuation method. The different levels have been defined as follows: – Quoted prices (unadjusted) in active markets for identical assets or liabilities (Level 1).

Notes to the consolidated financial statements

(All amounts in C thousands unless otherwise stated)

– Inputs other than quoted prices included within level 1 that are observable for the asset or liability, either directly (that is, as prices) or indirectly (that is, derived from prices) (Level 2).
– Inputs for the asset or liability that are not based on observable market data (that is, unobservable inputs) (Level 3).

IFRS 13p93(a), (b)

	Fair value measurements at 31 December 2013 using		
	Quoted prices in active markets for identical assets (Level 1)	Significant other observable inputs (Level 2)	Significant unobservable inputs (Level 3)
Recurring fair value measurements			
Land and buildings			
– Office buildings – UK	–	7,428	–
– Retail units – UK	–	19,027	–
– Retail units – US	–	14,200	–
– Manufacturing sites – UK	–	–	25,392
– Manufacturing sites – Asia Pacific	–	–	23,691

IFRS 13p93(c) There were no transfers between levels 1 and 2 during the year.

Valuation techniques used to derive level 2 fair values

IFRS 13p93(d) Level 2 fair values of land and retail units have been derived using the sales comparison approach. Sales prices of comparable land and buildings in close proximity are adjusted for differences in key attributes such as property size. The most significant input into this valuation approach is price per square foot.

IFRS 13p93(e) Fair value measurements using significant unobservable inputs (Level 3)

	Manufacturing sites – UK	Manufacturing sites – Asia Pacific
Opening balance	24,562	18,327
Transfers to/ (from) Level 3	–	3,434
Additions	1,489	1,651
Disposals	(1,100)	–
IFRS 13p93(e)(i) Gains and losses recognised in other comprehensive income	441	279
Closing balance	25,392	23,691

The Group commenced redevelopment of a factory in China during the year. The redevelopment will greatly expand the transport infrastructure of the factory, and is expected to be completed in 2014. Prior to redevelopment, this property was valued using the sales comparison approach, which resulted in a level 2 fair value. Upon redevelopment, the Group had to revise its valuation technique for the property under construction. The revised valuation technique uses significant unobservable inputs. Accordingly, the fair value was reclassified to level 3.

(All amounts in C thousands unless otherwise stated)

The revised valuation technique uses the sales comparison approach to derive the fair value of the completed property. The following were then deducted from the fair value of the completed property:
– estimated construction and other costs to completion that would be incurred by a market participant; and
– estimated profit margin that a market participant would require to hold and develop the property to completion, based on the state of the property as at 31 December 2013.

IFRS13p 93(c),(e)(iv) The group's policy is to recognise transfers into and transfers out of fair value hierarchy levels as of the date of the event or change in circumstances that caused the transfer.

IFRS13 p93g **Valuation processes of the group**

IFRS13 IE 65 The group's finance department includes a team that performs the valuations of land and buildings required for financial reporting purposes, including level 3 fair values. This team reports directly to the chief financial officer (CFO) and the audit committee (AC). Discussions of valuation processes and results are held between the CFO, AC and the valuation team at least once every quarter, in line with the group's quarterly reporting dates.

On an annual basis, the group engages external, independent and qualified valuers to determine the fair value of the group's land and buildings. As at 31 December 2013, the fair values of the land and buildings have been determined by XYZ Property Surveyors Limited.

The external valuations of the level 3 land and buildings have been performed using a sales comparison approach, similar to the level 2 land and buildings. However for manufacturing sites there have been a limited number of similar sales in the local market and the valuations have been performed using unobservable inputs. The external valuers, in discussion with the group's internal valuation team, has determined these inputs based on the size, age and condition of the land and buildings, the state of the local economy and comparable prices in the corresponding national economy.

The group has also valued land and buildings in China which is undergoing significant development of the transport infrastructure. The valuation has been performed using an adjusted sales comparison approach. The fair value of the completed land and buildings has been derived from observable sales prices of similar land and buildings in the local market. The estimated costs of completion, including a reasonable profit margin a market participant would require, has then been deducted to give estimate of the current fair value of the land and buildings.

Notes to the consolidated financial statements

(All amounts in C thousands unless otherwise stated)

IFRS 13p93(d),(h)(i)	Information about fair value measurements using significant unobservable inputs (Level 3)					
	Description	**Fair value at 31 December 2013**	**Valuation technique(s)**	**Unobservable inputs[1]**	**Range of unobservable inputs (probability – weighted average)**	**Relationship of unobservable inputs to fair value**
	Manufacturing sites – UK	25,392	Sales comparison approach	Price per square metre	C350-C470 (C400)	The higher the price per square metre, the higher the fair value
	Manufacturing sites – Asia Pacific	19,098	Sales comparison approach	Price per square metre	C235-C390 (C330)	The higher the price per square metre, the higher the fair value
		4,593	Adjusted sales comparison approach	Estimated costs to completion	C2,780,000-C3,220,000 (C2,900,000)	The higher the estimated costs, the lower the fair value.
				Estimated profit margin required to hold and develop property to completion	10%-15% (14%) of property value	The higher the profit margin required, the lower the fair value.

(All amounts in C thousands unless otherwise stated)

17 Intangible assets

	Cost	Goodwill	Trademarks and licences	Internally generated software develop-ment costs	Total
38p118(c)	At 1 January 2012 (Restated)	12,546	8,301	1,455	22,302
38p118(e)(vii)	Exchange differences	(546)	(306)	(45)	(897)
38p118(e)(i)	Additions	–	700	–	700
	As at 31 December 2012 (Restated)	12,000	8,695	1,410	22,105
38p118(e)(vii)	Exchange differences	341	96	134	571
38p118(e)(i)	Additions	–	684	2,366	3,050
38p118(e)(i)	Acquisition of subsidiary (note 39)	4,501	4,000	–	8,501
IFRS5p38	Transferred to disposal group classified as held for sale	(100)	(1,000)	–	(1,100)
	As at 31 December 2013	16,742	12,475	3,910	33,127
	Accumulated amortisation and impairment				
38p118(c)	At 1 January 2012	–	(330)	(510)	(840)
38p118(e)(vi)	Amortisation charge (note 9)	–	(365)	(200)	(565)
	As at 31 December 2012 (Restated)	–	(695)	(710)	(1,405)
38p118(e)(iv)	Impairment charge (note 9)	(4,650)	–	–	(4,650)
38p118(e)(vi)	Amortisation charge (note 9)	–	(680)	(120)	(800)
	As at 31 December 2013	(4,650)	(1,375)	(830)	(6,855)
	Net book value				
38p118(c)	Cost	12,000	8,695	1,410	22,105
38p118(c)	Accumulated amortisation and impairment	–	(695)	(710)	(1,405)
	As at 31 December 2012 (Restated)	12,000	8,000	700	20,700
38p118(c)	Cost	16,742	12,475	3,910	33,127
38p118(c)	Accumulated amortisation and impairment	(4,650)	(1,375)	(830)	(6,855)
	As at 31 December 2013	12,092	11,100	3,080	26,272

36p126(a) The carrying amount of the Russia wholesale segment has been reduced to its recoverable amount through recognition of an impairment loss against goodwill. This loss has been included in 'cost of sales' in the income statement.

38p118(d) Amortisation of C40 (2012: C100) is included in 'cost of sales' in the income statement; C680 (2012: C365) in 'distribution costs'; and C80 (2012: C100) in 'administrative expenses'.

DV The trademark transferred to the disposal group classified as held for sale relates to the Shoes Limited trademark (part of the wholesale segment), which was previously recognised by the group on the acquisition of the entity in 2007. A further net book amount of C100 transferred to the disposal group relates to goodwill. See note 25 for further details regarding the disposal group held for sale.

Notes to the consolidated financial statements

(All amounts in C thousands unless otherwise stated)

Impairment tests for goodwill

36p130(d)
Management reviews the business performance based on geography and type of business. It has identified UK, US, China, Russia and Europe as the main geographies. There are both retail and wholesale segments in the UK and the US. In all other geographies, the group has only wholesale business. Goodwill is monitored by the management at the operating segment level. The following is a summary of goodwill allocation for each operating segment:

36p134(a)

2013	Opening	Addition	Disposal	Impair-ment	Other adjust-ments	Closing
UK wholesale	6,075	–	(100)	–	215	6,190
UK retail	15	–	–	–	5	20
US wholesale	115	–	–	–	15	130
US retail	30	3,597	–	–	(55)	3,572
Europe wholesale	770	904	–	–	100	1,774
Russia wholesale	4,695	–	–	(4,650)	5	50
China wholesale	100	–	–	–	46	146
All other segments	200	–	–	–	10	210
Total	**12,000**	**4,501**	**(100)**	**(4,650)**	**341**	**12,092**

2012 (Restated)						
UK wholesale	6,370	–	–	–	(295)	6,075
UK retail	20	–	–	–	(5)	15
US wholesale	125	–	–	–	(10)	115
US retail	131	–	–	–	(101)	30
Europe wholesale	705	–	–	–	65	770
Russia wholesale	4,750	–	–	–	(55)	4,695
China wholesale	175	–	–	–	(75)	100
All other segments	270	–	–	–	(70)	200
Total	**12,546**	**–**	**–**	**–**	**(546)**	**12,000**

During 2012, US retail did not qualify as a reportable operating segment. However, with the acquisition in 2013 of ABC Group (note 39), US retail qualifies as a separate reportable segment, the comparatives have therefore been restated to be consistent.

36p130(e),
36p134(c),
36p134(d)(iii)
The recoverable amount of all CGUs has been determined based on value-in-use calculations. These calculations use pre-tax cash flow projections based on financial budgets approved by management covering a five-year period. Cash flows beyond the five-year period are extrapolated using the estimated growth rates stated below. The growth rate does not exceed the long-term average growth rate for the shoe business in which the CGU operates.

(All amounts in C thousands unless otherwise stated)

36p134(d)(i) The key assumptions used for value-in-use calculations in 2013 are as follows:[1]

		UK whole-sale	UK retail	US whole-sale	US retail	Europe whole-sale	Russia whole-sale	China whole-sale	All other segments
36p134(d)	Compound annual volume growth[2]	3.5%	4.3%	3.8%	4.1%	5.4%	6.2%	8.7%	4.4%
36p134(d)(iv)	Long term growth rate[3]	1.8%	2.1%	1.8%	2.3%	1.8%	2.0%	3.0%	3.9%
36p134(d)(v), 130(g)	Discount rate[4]	12.5%	13.0%	12.0%	12.5%	12.7%	13.8%	14.0%	14.8%
36p134(c)	Recoverable amount of the CGU						22,659		

36p134(d)(i) The key assumptions used for value-in-use calculations in 2012 are as follows:

		UK whole-sale	UK retail	US whole-sale	US retail	Europe whole-sale	Russia whole-sale	China whole-sale	All other segments
36p134(d)	Compound annual volume growth rate[2]	3.4%	4.5%	3.9%	4.1%	5.4%	5.8%	8.9%	3.8%
36p134 (d)(iv)	Long term growth rate[3]	2.0%	2.3%	2.0%	2.5%	2.0%	2.5%	3.5%	3.3%
36p134(d)(v), 36p130(g)	Discount rate[4]	12.0%	12.3%	11.5%	12.5%	12.1%	13.5%	14.5%	13.0%

Commentary – disclosure of recoverable amount

IFRS 13 amended IAS 36 paragraph 134 (c) to include the disclosure of the recoverable amount for CGUs with significant carrying amounts of goodwill. However the IASB indicated that this was not their intention and published an amendment to IAS 36 in May 2013 to remove the disclosure requirements. Disclosure of the recoverable amount will still be required for CGUs for which there has been an impairment loss during the period. The amendment is effective for annual periods starting on or after 1 January 2014, early adoption is permitted. IFRS plc has early adopted the amendment.

36p134(d)(ii) These assumptions have been used for the analysis of each CGU within the operating segment.

[1] Disclosure of long-term growth rates and discount rates is required. Other key assumptions are required to be disclosed and quantified where a reasonably possible change in the key assumption would remove any remaining headroom in the impairment calculation. Otherwise the additional disclosures are encouraged but not required.
[2] Compound annual volume growth rate in the initial five-year period
[3] Weighted average growth rate used to extrapolate cash flows beyond the budget period.
[4] Pre-tax discount rate applied to the cash flow projections.

Notes to the consolidated financial statements

(All amounts in C thousands unless otherwise stated)

36p134(d)(ii) Management determined compound annual volume growth rate for each CGU covering over the five-year forecast period to be a key assumption. The volume of sales in each period is the main driver for revenue and costs. The compound annual volume growth rate is based on past performance and management's expectations of market development. The long term growth rates used are consistent with the forecasts included in industry reports. The discount rates used are pre-tax and reflect specific risks relating to the relevant operating segments.

36p130(a) The impairment charge arose in a wholesale CGU in Step-land (included in the Russian operating segment) following a decision in early 2013 to reduce the manufacturing output allocated to these operations (note 35). This was a result of a redefinition of the group's allocation of manufacturing volumes across all CGUs in order to benefit from advantageous market conditions. Following this decision, the group reassessed the depreciation policies of its property, plant and equipment in this country and estimated that their useful lives would not be affected. No class of asset other than goodwill was impaired. The pre-tax discount rate used in the previous years for the wholesale CGU in Step-land was 13.5%.

36p134(f) In European Wholesale, the recoverable amount calculated based on value in use exceeded carrying value by C705. A compound annual volume growth rate of 1.5%, a fall in long term growth rate to 1.6% or a rise in discount rate to 14.9% would remove the remaining headroom.

(All amounts in C thousands unless otherwise stated)

18 Financial instruments

18(a) Financial instruments by category

IFRS7p6

31 December 2013

	Loans and receivables	Assets at fair value through profit and loss	Derivatives used for hedging	Available for sale	Total
Assets as per balance sheet					
Available-for-sale financial assets	–	–	–	19,370	19,370
Derivative financial instruments	–	361	1,103	–	1,464
Trade and other receivables excluding pre-payments[1]	20,837	–	–	–	20,837
Financial assets at fair value through profit or loss	–	11,820	–	–	11,820
Cash and cash equivalents	17,928	–	–	–	17,928
Total	**38,765**	**12,181**	**1,103**	**19,370**	**71,419**

	Liabilities at fair value through profit and loss	Derivatives used for hedging	Other financial liabilities at amortised cost	Total
Liabilities as per balance sheet				
Borrowings (excluding finance lease liabilities)	–	–	117,839	117,839
Finance lease liabilities[2]	–	–	8,998	8,998
Derivative financial instruments	268	327	–	595
Trade and other payables excluding non-financial liabilities[3]	–	–	15,668	15,668
Total	**268**	**327**	**142,505**	**143,100**

31 December 2012 (Restated)

	Loans and receivables	Assets at fair value through profit and loss	Derivatives used for hedging	Available for sale	Total
Assets as per balance sheet					
Available-for-sale financial assets	–	–	–	14,910	14,910
Derivative financial instruments	–	321	875	–	1,196
Trade and other receivables excluding pre-payments[1]	18,576	–	–	–	18,576
Financial assets at fair value through profit or loss	–	7,972	–	–	7,972
Cash and cash equivalents	34,062	–	–	–	34,062
Total	**52,638**	**8,293**	**875**	**14,910**	**76,716**

[1] Pre-payments are excluded from the trade and other receivables balance, as this analysis is required only for financial instruments.
[2] The categories in this disclosure are determined by IAS 39. Finance leases are mostly outside the scope of IAS 39, but they remain within the scope of IFRS 7. Therefore finance leases have been shown separately.
[3] Non-financial liabilities are excluded from the trade payables balance, as this analysis is required only for financial instruments.

Notes to the consolidated financial statements

(All amounts in C thousands unless otherwise stated)

	Liabilities at fair value through profit and loss	Derivatives used for hedging	Other financial liabilities at amortised cost	Total
Liabilities as per balance sheet				
Borrowings (excluding finance lease liabilities)	–	–	104,006	104,006
Finance lease liabilities[1]	–	–	10,598	10,598
Derivative financial instruments	298	449	–	747
Trade and other payables excluding non-financial liabilities	–	–	11,518	11,518
Total	298	449	126,122	126,869

[1] The categories in this disclosure are determined by IAS 39. Finance leases are mostly outside the scope of IAS 39, but they remain within the scope of IFRS 7. Therefore finance leases have been shown separately.

(All amounts in C thousands unless otherwise stated)

18(b) Credit quality of financial assets

IFRS7p36(c)   The credit quality of financial assets that are neither past due nor impaired can be assessed by reference to external credit ratings (if available) or to historical information about counterparty default rates:

	2013	2012
		Restated
Trade receivables		
Counterparties with external credit rating (Moody's)		
A	5,895	5,757
BB	3,200	3,980
BBB	1,500	1,830
	10,595	11,567
Counterparties without external credit rating:		
Group 1	750	555
Group 2	4,832	3,596
Group 3	1,770	1,312
	7,352	5,463
Total unimpaired trade receivables	17,947	17,030
Cash at bank and short-term bank deposits[1]		
AAA	8,790	15,890
AA	5,300	7,840
A	3,038	9,832
	17,128	33,562
DV **Available-for-sale debt securities**		
AA	347	264
	347	264
DV **Derivative financial assets**		
AAA	1,046	826
AA	418	370
	1,464	1,196
Loans to related parties		
Group 2	2,501	1,301
Group 3	167	87
	2,668	1,388

Group 1 – new customers/related parties (less than 6 months).
Group 2 – existing customers/related parties (more than 6 months) with no defaults in the past.
Group 3 – existing customers/related parties (more than 6 months) with some defaults in the past. All defaults were fully recovered.

None of the loans to related parties is past due but not impaired.

---

[1] The rest of the balance sheet item 'cash and cash equivalents' is cash in hand.

Notes to the consolidated financial statements

(All amounts in C thousands unless otherwise stated)

19 Available-for-sale financial assets

	2013	2012
At 1 January	**14,910**	13,222
Exchange differences	646	(435)
Acquisition of subsidiary (note 39)	473	–
Additions	4,887	1,150
Disposals	(106)	–
Transfer on account of acquisition of control	(1,150)	–
Net gains/(losses) transfer from equity (note 29)	(980)	(152)
Net gains/(losses) transfer to equity (note 29)	690	1,125
At 31 December	**19,370**	**14,910**
Less non-current portion	**(17,420)**	**(14,910)**
Current portion	**1,950**	**–**

1p79(b)
1p66,1p69
1p66,1p69

IFRS7p20(a)(ii) The group removed profits of C217 (2012: C187) and losses C87 (2012: C35) from equity into the income statement. Losses in the amount of C55 (2012: C20) were due to impairments.

Available-for-sale financial assets include the following:

IFRS7p31, 34

	2013	2012
Listed securities:		
Equity securities – UK	8,335	8,300
Equity securities – Europe	5,850	2,086
Equity securities – US	4,550	4,260
Debentures with fixed interest of 6.5% and maturity date of 27 August 2015	210	–
Non cumulative 9% non-redeemable preference shares	78	–
Unlisted securities:		
Debt securities with fixed interest ranging from 6.3% to 6.5% and maturity dates between July 2014 and May 2016	347	264
Total	**19,370**	**14,910**

IFRS7p34(c) Available-for-sale financial assets are denominated in the following currencies:

	2013	2012
UK pound	8,335	8,300
Euro	5,850	2,086
US dollar	4,550	4,260
Other currencies	635	264
Total	**19,370**	**14,910**

IFRS7p27 The fair values of unlisted securities are based on cash flows discounted using a rate based on the market interest rate and the risk premium specific to the unlisted securities (2013: 6%; 2012: 5.8%).

IFRS7p36(a) The maximum exposure to credit risk at the reporting date is the carrying value of the debt securities classified as available for sale.

IFRS7p36(c) None of these financial assets is either past due or impaired.

(All amounts in C thousands unless otherwise stated)

20 Derivative financial instruments

		2013		2012	
		Assets	**Liabilities**	Assets	Liabilities
IFRS7p22(a)(b)	Interest rate swaps – cash flow hedge	351	110	220	121
IFRS7p22(a)(b)	Interest rate swaps – fair value hedges	57	37	49	11
IFRS7p22(a)(b)	Forward foreign exchange contracts – cash flow hedges	695	180	606	317
	Forward foreign exchange contracts – held-for-trading	361	268	321	298
	Total	**1,464**	**595**	**1,196**	**747**
1p66, p69	Less non-current portion:				
	Interest rate swaps – cash flow hedges	345	100	200	120
	Interest rate swaps– fair value hedges	50	35	45	9
		395	135	245	129
1p66, p69	**Current portion**	**1,069**	**460**	951	618

Trading derivatives are classified as a current asset or liability. The full fair value of a hedging derivative is classified as a non-current asset or liability if the remaining maturity of the hedged item is more than 12 months and, as a current asset or liability, if the maturity of the hedged item is less than 12 months.

IFRS7p24 The ineffective portion recognised in the profit or loss that arises from fair value hedges amounts to a loss of C1 (2012: loss of C1) (note 8). The ineffective portion recognised in the profit or loss that arises from cash flow hedges amounts to a gain of C17 (2012: a gain of C14) (note 8). There was no ineffectiveness to be recorded from net investment in foreign entity hedges.

(a) Forward foreign exchange contracts

IFRS7p31 The notional principal amounts of the outstanding forward foreign exchange contracts at 31 December 2013 were C92,370 (2012: C89,689).

IFRS7p23(a), 39p100, 1p79(b) The hedged highly probable forecast transactions denominated in foreign currency are expected to occur at various dates during the next 12 months. Gains and losses recognised in the hedging reserve in equity (note 29) on forward foreign exchange contracts as of 31 December 2013 are recognised in the income statement in the period or periods during which the hedged forecast transaction affects the income statement. This is generally within 12 months of the end of the reporting period unless the gain or loss is included in the initial amount recognised for the purchase of fixed assets, in which case recognition is over the lifetime of the asset (5 to 10 years).

(b) Interest rate swaps

IFRS7p31 The notional principal amounts of the outstanding interest rate swap contracts at 31 December 2013 were C4,314 (2012: C3,839).

IFRS7p23(a), 1p79(b) At 31 December 2013, the fixed interest rates vary from 6.9% to 7.4% (2012: 6.7% to 7.2%), and the main floating rates are EURIBOR and LIBOR. Gains and losses recognised in the hedging reserve in equity (note 29) on interest rate swap contracts as of 31 December 2013 will be continuously released to the income statement within finance cost until the repayment of the bank borrowings (note 31).

Notes to the consolidated financial statements

(All amounts in C thousands unless otherwise stated)

(c) Hedge of net investment in foreign entity

IFRS7p22,
1p79(b)

A proportion of the group's US dollar-denominated borrowing amounting to C321 (2012: C321) is designated as a hedge of the net investment in the group's US subsidiary. The fair value of the borrowing at 31 December 2013 was C370 (2012: C279). The foreign exchange loss of C45 (2012: gain of C40) on translation of the borrowing to currency at the end of the reporting period is recognised in other comprehensive income.

IFRS7p36(a) The maximum exposure to credit risk at the reporting date is the fair value of the derivative assets in the balance sheet.

21 Trade and other receivables

		2013	2012 Restated
IFRS7p36, **1p77**	Trade receivables	**18,174**	17,172
	Less: provision for impairment of trade receivables	**(109)**	(70)
1p78(b)	Trade receivables - net	**18,065**	17,102
1p78(b)	Prepayments	**1,250**	1,106
24p18(b), **1p78(b)**	Receivables from related parties (note 41)	**104**	86
24p18(b),	Loans to related parties (note 41)	**2,668**	1,388
		22,087	19,682
1p78(b),1p66	Less non-current portion: loans to related parties	**(2,322)**	(1,352)
1p66	**Current portion**	**19,765**	18,330

All non-current receivables are due within five years from the end of the reporting period.

The fair values of trade and other receivables are as follows:

IFRS7p25

	2013	2012 Restated
Trade receivables	**18,065**	17,102
Receivables from related parties	**104**	86
Loans to related parties	**2,722**	1,398
	20,891	18,586

IFRS13p **93(b),(d),** **IFRS13p97** The fair values of loans to related parties are based on cash flows discounted using a rate based on the borrowings rate of 7.5% (2012: 7.2%). The discount rate equals to LIBOR plus appropriate credit rating. The fair values are within level 2 of the fair value hierarchy.

(All amounts in C thousands unless otherwise stated)

24p18(b)(i) The effective interest rates on non-current receivables were as follows:

	2013	2012
Loans to related parties (note 41)	6.5-7%	6.5-7%

IFRS7p14 Certain European subsidiaries of the group transferred receivable balances amounting to C1,014 to a bank in exchange for cash during the year ended 31 December 2013. The transaction has been accounted for as a collateralised borrowing (note 31). In case the entities default under the loan agreement, the bank has the right to receive the cash flows from the receivables transferred. Without default, the entities will collect the receivables and allocate new receivables as collateral.

DV As of 31 December 2013, trade receivables of C17,670 (2012: C16,823) were fully performing.

IFRS7p37(a) As of 31 December 2013, trade receivables of C277 (2012: C207) were past due but not impaired. These relate to a number of independent customers for whom there is no recent history of default. The ageing analysis of these trade receivables is as follows:

	2013	2012 Restated
Up to 3 months	177	108
3 to 6 months	100	99
	277	207

IFRS7p37(b) As of 31 December 2013, trade receivables of C227 (2012: C142) were impaired. The amount of the provision was C109 as of 31 December 2013 (2012: C70). The individually impaired receivables mainly relate to wholesalers, which are in unexpectedly difficult economic situations. It was assessed that a portion of the receivables is expected to be recovered. The ageing of these receivables is as follows:

	2013	2012 Restated
3 to 6 months	177	108
Over 6 months	50	34
	227	142

The carrying amounts of the group's trade and other receivables are denominated in the following currencies:

	2013	2012 Restated
UK pound	9,846	8,669
Euros	5,987	6,365
US dollar	6,098	4,500
Other currencies	156	148
	22,087	19,682

(All amounts in C thousands unless otherwise stated)

IFRS7p16 Movements on the group provision for impairment of trade receivables are as follows:

	2013	2012 Restated
At 1 January	70	38
Provision for receivables impairment	74	61
Receivables written off during the year as uncollectible	(28)	(23)
Unused amounts reversed	(10)	(8)
Unwind of discount	3	2
At 31 December	**109**	70

IFRS7p20(e) *(marginal reference against "Provision for receivables impairment" row)*

The creation and release of provision for impaired receivables have been included in 'other expenses' in the income statement (note 9a). Unwind of discount is included in 'finance costs' in the income statement (note 11). Amounts charged to the allowance account are generally written off, when there is no expectation of recovering additional cash.

IFRS7p16 The other classes within trade and other receivables do not contain impaired assets.

IFRS7p36(a) The maximum exposure to credit risk at the reporting date is the carrying value of each class of receivables mentioned above. The group does not hold any collateral as security.

22 Inventories

	2013	2012 Restated
Raw materials	7,622	7,612
Work in progress	1,810	1,796
Finished goods[1]	15,268	8,774
	24,700	18,182

2p36(b), 1p78(c) *(marginal reference against "Raw materials" row)*

2p36(d), p38 The cost of inventories recognised as an expense and included in 'cost of sales' amounted to C60,252 (2012:C29,545).

2p36(f-g) The group reversed C603 of a previous inventory write-down in July 2013. The group has sold all the goods that were written down to an independent retailer in Australia at original cost. The amount reversed has been included in 'cost of sales' in the income statement.

---

[1] Separate disclosure of finished goods at fair value less cost to sell is required, where applicable.

(All amounts in C thousands unless otherwise stated)

23 Financial assets at fair value through profit or loss

	2013	2012
IFRS7p8(a), Listed securities – held for trading		
p31, p34(c)		
– Equity securities – UK	**5,850**	3,560
– Equity securities – Europe	**4,250**	3,540
– Equity securities – US	**1,720**	872
	11,820	7,972

7p15   Financial assets at fair value through profit or loss are presented within 'operating activities' as part of changes in working capital in the statement of cash flows (note 36).

IFRS7p20   Changes in fair values of financial assets at fair value through profit or loss are recorded in 'other (losses)/gains – net' in the income statement (note 8).

IFRS13p91   The fair value of all equity securities is based on their current bid prices in an active market.

24 Cash and cash equivalents

	2013	2012 Restated
Cash at bank and in hand	**8,398**	28,648
Short-term bank deposits	**9,530**	5,414
Cash and cash equivalents (excluding bank overdrafts)	**17,928**	34,062

7p45   Cash and cash equivalents include the following for the purposes of the statement of cash flows:

	2013	2012 Restated
Cash and cash equivalents	**17,928**	34,062
7p8 Bank overdrafts (note 31)	**(2,650)**	(6,464)
Cash and cash equivalents	**15,278**	27,598

Notes to the consolidated financial statements

(All amounts in C thousands unless otherwise stated)

25 Non-current assets held for sale and discontinued operations

IFRS5p41
(a)(b)(d)
The assets and liabilities related to Shoes Limited (part of the UK wholesale segment) have been presented as held for sale following the approval of the group's management and shareholders on 23 September 2013 to sell Shoes Limited in the UK. The completion date for the transaction is expected by May 2014.

		2013	2012
IFRS5p33(c)	Operating cash flows[1]	300	190
IFRS5p33(c)	Investing cash flows[1]	(103)	(20)
IFRS5p33(c)	Financing cash flows[1]	(295)	(66)
	Total cash flows	(98)	104

IFRS5p38
(a) Assets of disposal group classified as held for sale

	2013	2012
Property, plant and equipment	1,563	–
Goodwill	100	–
Other intangible assets	1,000	–
Inventory	442	–
Other current assets	228	–
Total	3,333	–

IFRS5p38
(b) Liabilities of disposal group classified as held for sale

	2013	2012
Trade and other payables	104	–
Other current liabilities	20	–
Provisions	96	–
Total	220	–

IFRS13p
93(a),(b),(d)
In accordance with IFRS 5, the assets and liabilities held for sale were written down to their fair value less costs to sell of C3,113,000. This is a non-recurring fair value which has been measured using observable inputs, being the prices for recent sales of similar businesses, and is therefore within level 2 of the fair value hierarchy. The fair value has been measured by calculating the ratio of transaction price to annual revenue for the similar businesses and applying the average to Shoes Limited.

---

[1] Under this approach, the entity presents the statement of cash flows as if no discontinued operation has occurred and makes the required IFRS5p33 disclosures in the notes. It would also be acceptable to present the three categories separately on the face of the statement of cash flows and present the line-by-line breakdown of the categories, either in the notes or on the face of the statement of cash flows. It would not be acceptable to present all cash flows from discontinued operations in one line either as investing or operating activity.

(All amounts in C thousands unless otherwise stated)

IFRS5p33(b)   Analysis of the result of discontinued operations,[1] and the result recognised on the re-measurement of assets or disposal group is as follows:[2]

		2013	2012
Revenue		**1,200**	1,150
Expenses		**(960)**	(950)
Profit before tax of discontinued operations		**240**	200
12p81(h)(ii) Tax		**(96)**	(80)
Profit after tax of discontinued operations		**144**	120
Pre-tax gain/(loss) recognised on the re-measurement of assets of disposal group		**(73)**	–
12p81(h)(ii) Tax		**29**	–
After tax gain/(loss) recognised on the re-measurement of assets of disposal group		**(44)**	–
Profit for the year from discontinued operations		**100**	120

26 Share capital and premium

		Number of shares (thousands)	Ordinary shares	Share premium	Total
	At 1 January 2012	20,000	20,000	10,424	30,424
1p106(d)(iii)	Employee share option scheme: – Proceeds from shares issued	1,000	1,000	70	1,070
	At 31 December 2012	21,000	21,000	10,494	31,494
1p106(d)(iii)	Employee share option scheme: – Proceeds from shares issued	750	750	200	950
IFRS3p B64(f)(iv)	Acquisition of subsidiary (note 39)	3,550	3,550	6,450	10,000
1p79(a)	**At 31 December 2013**	**25,300**	**25,300**	**17,144**	**42,444**

1p79(a)   The company acquired 875,000 of its own shares through purchases on the EuroMoney stock exchange on 18 April 2013. The total amount paid to acquire the shares, net of income tax, was C2,564. The shares are held as 'treasury shares'.[3] The company has the right to re-issue these shares at a later date. All shares issued by the company were fully paid.

The group issued 3,550,000 shares on 1 March 2013 14% of the total ordinary share capital issued) to the shareholders of ABC Group as part of the purchase consideration for 70% of its ordinary share capital. The ordinary shares issued have the same rights as the other shares in issue. The fair value of the shares issued amounted to C10,050 (C2.83 per share). The related transaction costs amounting to C50 have been netted off with the deemed proceeds.

---

[1] IFRS 5 requires the separate presentation of any cumulative income or expense recognised in other comprehensive income relating to a non-current asset (or disposal group) classified as held for sale. There are no items recognised in equity relating to the disposal group classified as held-for-sale.
[2] These disclosures can also be given in the primary financial statements.
[3] Treasury shares should be accounted for in accordance with local company law and practice. Treasury shares may be disclosed separately on the balance sheet or deducted from retained earnings or a specific reserve. Depending on local company law, the company could have the right to resell the treasury shares.

Notes to the consolidated financial statements

(All amounts in C thousands unless otherwise stated)

27 Share-based payments

IFRS2p45(a) Share options are granted to directors and to selected employees. The exercise price of the granted options is equal to the market price of the shares less 15% on the date of the grant. Options are conditional on the employee completing three years' service (the vesting period). The options are exercisable starting three years from the grant date, subject to the group achieving its target growth in earnings per share over the period of inflation plus 4%, the options have a contractual option term of five years. The group has no legal or constructive obligation to repurchase or settle the options in cash.

Movements in the number of share options outstanding and their related weighted average exercise prices are as follows:

		2013		2012	
		Average exercise price in C per share option	Options (thousands)	Average exercise price in C per share option	Options (thousands)
IFRS2p45(b)(i)	At 1 January	1.73	4,744	1.29	4,150
IFRS2p45(b)(ii)	Granted	2.95	964	2.38	1,827
IFRS2p 45(b)(iii)	Forfeited	2.30	(125)	0.80	(33)
IFRS2p 45(b)(iv)	Exercised	1.28	(750)	1.08	(1,000)
IFRS2p45(b) (v)	Expired	0.00	–	2.00	(200)
IFRS2p 45(b)(vi)	**At 31 December**	2.03	4,833	1.73	4,744

IFRS2p45 (b)(vii), IFRS2p45(c) Out of the 4,833,000 outstanding options (2012: 4,744,000 options), 1,875,000 options (2012: 1,400,000) were exercisable. Options exercised in 2013 resulted in 750,000 shares (2012: 1,000,000 shares) being issued at a weighted average price of C1.28 each (2012: C1.08 each). The related weighted average share price at the time of exercise was C2.85 (2012: C2.65) per share. The related transaction costs amounting to C10 (2012: C10) have been netted off with the proceeds received.

IFRS2p45(d) Share options outstanding at the end of the year have the following expiry date and exercise prices:

Grant-vest	Expiry date – 1 July	Exercise price in C per share options	Share options (thousands)	
			2013	2012
2008-11	2013	1.10	–	500
2009-12	2014	1.20	800	900
2010-13	2015	1.35	1,075	1,250
2011-14	2016	2.00	217	267
2012-15	2017	2.38	1,777	1,827
2013-16	2018	2.95	964	–
			4,833	4,744

(All amounts in C thousands unless otherwise stated)

IFRS2p46, p47(a) The weighted average fair value of options granted during the period determined using the Black-Scholes valuation model was C0.86 per option (2012: C0.66). The significant inputs into the model were weighted average share price of C3.47 (2012: C2.80) at the grant date, exercise price shown above, volatility of 30% (2012: 27%), dividend yield of 4.3% (2012: 3.5%), an expected option life of three years (2012: 3 years) and an annual risk-free interest rate of 5% (2012: 4%). The volatility measured at the standard deviation of continuously compounded share returns is based on statistical analysis of daily share prices over the last three years. See note 10 for the total expense recognised in the income statement for share options granted to directors and employees.

28 Retained earnings

1p106(d)	At 1 January 2012 (Restated)	51,125
	Profit for the year	16,304
1p106(d)	Dividends paid relating to 2011	(15,736)
IFRS2p50	Value of employee services[1]	822
16p41	Depreciation transfer on land and buildings net of tax	87
12p68C	Tax credit relating to share option scheme	20
19Rp120(c)	Remeasurements of post employment benefit liabilities net of tax	(637)
	At 31 December 2012 (Restated)	51,985
1p106(d)	At 1 January 2013	51,985
	Profit for the year	31,874
1p106(d)	Dividends paid relating to 2012	(10,102)
IFRS2p50	Value of employee services[1]	690
16p41	Depreciation transfer on land and buildings net of tax	80
	Revaluation transfer on disposal of land and buildings	20
12p68C	Tax credit relating to share option scheme	30
19Rp120(c)	Remeasurements of post employment benefit liabilities net of tax	83
12p81(a),(b)	Impact of change in Euravian tax rate on deferred tax	(10)
	At 31 December 2013	**74,650**

[1] The credit entry to equity in respect of the IFRS 2 charge should be recorded in accordance with local company law and practice. This may be a specific reserve, retained earnings or share capital.

(All amounts in C thousands unless otherwise stated)

29 Other reserves

		Note	Convertible bond	Land and buildings revaluation[1]	Hedging	Treasury shares	Available-for-sale investments	Translation	Transactions with non-controlling interests	Total
	At 1 January 2012 (Restated)		–	1,152	65	–	1,320	3,827	–	6,364
16p39, 12p61A, 12p81(ae)	Revaluation of land and buildings – gross	16	–	1,133	–	–	–	–	–	1,133
12p61A, 12p81(ae)	Revaluation of land and buildings – tax	13	–	(374)	–	–	–	–	–	(374)
16p41	Depreciation transfer – gross		–	(130)	–	–	–	–	–	(130)
12p61A, 12p81(ae)	Depreciation transfer – tax		–	43						43
16p39, IFRS7p20 (a)(ii)	Revaluation of AFS – gross		–	–	–	–	1,125	–	–	1,125
16p39, IFRS7p20 (a)(ii)	Revaluation transfer AFS – gross	19	–	–	–	–	(152)	–	–	(152)
12p61A, 12p81(ae)	Revaluation of AFS – tax	13	–	–	–	–	(61)	–	–	(61)
28p39	Revaluation – associates	12	–	–	–	–	(14)	–	–	(14)
IFRS7p23(c)	Cash flow hedge: – Fair value gains in year		–	–	300	–	–	–	–	300
12p61,81 (ae)	– Tax on fair value gains	13	–	–	(101)	–	–	–	–	(101)
IFRS7p23(d)	– Transfers to sales		–	–	(236)	–	–	–	–	(236)
12p61A, 81 (ae)	– Tax on transfer to sales		–	–	79	–	–	–	–	79
IFRS7p23(e)	- Transfers to inventory		–	–	(67)	–	–	–	–	(67)
12p61, 12p81(ae)	– Tax on transfer to inventory	13	–	–	22	–	–	–	–	22
39p102(a)	Net investment hedge	20	–	–	–	–	–	40	–	40
21p52(b)	Currency translation differences – Group		–	–	–	–	–	(882)	–	(882)
28p39	Currency translation differences – Associates	12	–	–	–	–	–	105	–	105
	At 31 December 2012 (Restated)		–	1,824	62	–	2,218	3,090	–	7,194
16p39, 12p61A, 12p81(ae)	Revaluation of land and buildings – gross	16		1,005	–	–	–	–	–	1,005
12p61A, 12p81(ae)	Revaluation of land and buildings- tax	13	–	(250)	–	–	–	–	–	(250)
16p41	Depreciation transfer – gross		–	(129)	–	–	–	–	–	(129)

[1] An entity should disclose in its financial statements whether there are any restrictions on the distribution of the 'land and buildings' fair value reserve to the equity holders of the company (IAS16p77(f)).

(All amounts in C thousands unless otherwise stated)

		Note	Convertible bond	Land and buildings revaluation	Hedging	Treasury shares	Available-for-sale investments	Translation	Transactions with non-controlling interests	Total
12p61A, 12p81(ae)	Depreciation transfer – tax		–	49	–	–	–	–	–	49
	Disposal of land and buildings		–	(20)	–	–	–	–	–	(20)
16p39, IFRS7p20 (a)(ii)	Revaluation of AFS – gross	19	–	–	–	–	690	–	–	690
16p39, IFRS7p20 (a)(ii)	Revaluation transfer AFS – gross	19	–	–	–	–	(130)	–	–	(130)
12p61A, 12p81(ae)	Revaluation of AFS – tax	13	–	–	–	–	(198)	–		(198)
28p39	Revaluation – associates	12	–	–	–	–	(12)	–		(12)
IFRS7p23(c)	Cash flow hedge: – Fair value gains in year		–	–	368	–	–	–	–	368
12p61,81 (ae)	– Tax on fair value gains	13	–	–	(123)	–	–	–	–	(123)
IFRS7p23(d)	– Transfers to sales		–	–	(120)	–	–	–	–	(120)
12p61A, 81 (ae)	– Tax on transfers to sales	13	–	–	40	–	–	–	–	40
IFRS7p23(e)	– Transfers to inventory		–	–	(151)	–	–	–	–	(151)
12p61, 12p81(ae)	– Tax on transfers to inventory	13	–	–	50	–	–	–	–	50
39p102(a)	Net investment hedge	20	–	–	–	–	–	(45)	–	(45)
21p52(b)	Currency translation differences – Group		–	–	–	–	–	2,149	–	2,149
28p39	Currency translation differences – Associates	12	–	–	–	–	–	(74)	–	(74)
28p39	Convertible bond – equity component	31	7,761	–	–	–	–	–	–	7,761
12p61A, 12p81(ae)	Tax on convertible bond[1]	13	(2,328)	–	–	–	–	–	–	(2,328)
	Purchase of treasury shares		–	–	–	(2,564)	–	–	–	(2,564)
1p106(d) (iii)	Acquisition of non-controlling interest in XYZ Group		–	–	–	–	–	–	(800)	(800)
1p106(d) (iii)	Decrease in ownership interest in Red Limited		–	–	–	–	–	–	100	100
IFRS3p59	Reclassification of revaluation of previously held interest in ABC Group		–	–	–	–	(850)	–	–	(850)
	At 31 December 2013		**5,433**	**2,479**	**126**	**(2,564)**	**1,718**	**5,120**	**(700)**	**11,612**

[1] Temporary taxable difference for the liability component of the convertible bond in accordance with paragraph 23 of IAS 12. It is assumed that the tax base on the convertible bond is not split between the debt and equity elements. If the tax base were split, this would impact the deferred tax position.

Notes to the consolidated financial statements

(All amounts in C thousands unless otherwise stated)

Other comprehensive income, net of tax

		Other reserves	Retained earnings	Total	Non-controlling interests	Total other compre-hensive income
DV	**31 December 2013** **Items that will not be reclassified to profit or loss**					
16p39	Gains on revaluation of land and buildings	755	–	755	–	755
19p93A	Remeasurement of post employment benefit obligations	–	83	83	–	83
DV		755	83	838	–	838
DV	**Items that may be subsequently reclassified to profit or loss** Change in value of available-for-sale financial assets	362	–	362	–	362
IFRS3p59	Reclassification of revaluation of previously held interest in ABC Group	(850)	–	(850)	–	(850)
	Share of other comprehensive income of associates	(86)	–	(86)	–	(86)
	Impact of change in Euravian tax rate on deferred tax	–	(10)	(10)	–	(10)
	Cash flow hedges	64	–	64	–	64
39p102(a)	Net investment hedge	(45)	–	(45)	–	(45)
21p52(b)	Currency translation differences	2,149	–	2,149	252	2,401
	Depreciation on land and buildings	(100)	100	–	–	–
DV		1,494	90	1,584	252	1,836
	Total	2,249	173	2,422	252	2,674
DV	31 December 2012 (Restated) **Items that will not be reclassified to profit or loss**					
16p39	Gains on revaluation of land and buildings	759	–	759	–	759
19p93A	Remeasurement of post employment benefit obligations	–	(637)	(637)	–	(637)
DV		759	(637)	122	–	122
DV	**Items that may be subsequently reclassified to profit or loss** Change in value of available-for-sale financial assets	912	–	912	–	912
28p39	Share of other comprehensive income of associates	91	–	91	–	91
	Cash flow hedges	(3)	–	(3)	–	(3)
39p102(a)	Net investment hedge	40	–	40	–	40
21p52(b)	Currency translation differences	(882)	–	(882)	(40)	(922)
	Depreciation on land and buildings	(87)	87	–	–	–
DV		71	87	158	(40)	118
	Total	830	(550)	280	(40)	240

(All amounts in C thousands unless otherwise stated)

30 Trade and other payables

	Note	2013	2012 Restated
Trade payables		**8,983**	9,495
Amounts due to related parties	41	**3,202**	1,195
Social security and other taxes		**1,502**	960
Other liabilities – contingent consideration	39	**1,500**	–
Accrued expenses		**1,483**	828
		16,670	12,478

1p77 / 24p18

31 Borrowings

	2013	2012 Restated
Non-current		
Bank borrowings	**32,193**	40,244
Convertible bond	**42,822**	–
Debentures and other loans	**3,300**	18,092
Redeemable preference shares	**30,000**	30,000
Finance lease liabilities	**6,806**	8,010
	115,121	96,346
Current		
Bank overdraft (note 24)	**2,650**	6,464
Collaterised borrowings	**1,014**	–
Bank borrowings	**3,368**	4,598
Debentures and other loans	**2,492**	4,608
Finance lease liabilities	**2,192**	2,588
	11,716	18,258
Total borrowings	**126,837**	114,604

(a) Bank borrowings

IFRS7p31 Bank borrowings mature until 2017 and bear average coupons of 7.5% annually (2012: 7.4% annually).

IFRS7p14 Total borrowings include secured liabilities (bank and collateralised borrowings) of C37,680 (2012: C51,306). Bank borrowings are secured by the land and buildings of the group (note 16). Collateralised borrowings are secured by trade receivables (note 21).

Notes to the consolidated financial statements

(All amounts in C thousands unless otherwise stated)

IFRS7p31 The exposure of the group's borrowings to interest rate changes and the contractual re-pricing dates at the end of the reporting period are as follows:

	2013	2012 Restated
6 months or less	10,496	16,748
6-12 months	36,713	29,100
1-5 years	47,722	38,555
Over 5 years	31,906	30,201
	126,837	114,604

The carrying amounts and fair value of the non-current borrowings are as follows:

IFRS7p25

	Carrying amount		Fair value	
	2013	2012 Restated	2013	2012 Restated
Bank borrowings	32,193	40,244	32,590	39,960
Redeemable preference shares	30,000	30,000	28,450	28,850
Debentures and other loans	3,300	18,092	3,240	17,730
Convertible bond	42,822	–	42,752	–
Finance lease liabilities	6,806	8,010	6,205	7,990
Total	115,121	96,346	113,237	94,530

IFRS13p93(b), (d), IFRS13p97, IFRS7p25 The fair value of current borrowings equals their carrying amount, as the impact of discounting is not significant. The fair values are based on cash flows discounted using a rate based on the borrowing rate of 7.5% (2012: 7.2%) and are within level 2 of the fair value hierarchy.

IFRS7p31, IFRS7p34(c) The carrying amounts of the group's borrowings are denominated in the following currencies:

	2013	2012 Restated
UK pound	80,100	80,200
Euro	28,353	16,142
US dollar	17,998	17,898
Other currencies	386	364
Total	126,837	114,604

7p50(a) DV The group has the following undrawn borrowing facilities:

	2013	2012 Restated
Floating rate:		
Expiring within one year	6,150	4,100
Expiring beyond one year	14,000	8,400
Fixed rate:		
Expiring within one year	18,750	12,500
Total	38,900	25,000

(All amounts in C thousands unless otherwise stated)

IFRS7p17,
1p79(b)
The facilities expiring within one year are annual facilities subject to review at various dates during 2013. The other facilities have been arranged to help finance the proposed expansion of the group's activities in Europe.

(b) Convertible bonds

32p28, 32p31,
1p79(b)
The company issued 500,000 5.0% convertible bonds at a par value of C50 million[1] on 2 January 2013. The bonds mature five years from the issue date at their nominal value of C50 million or can be converted into shares at the holder's option at the maturity date at the rate of 33 shares per C5,000. The values of the liability component and the equity conversion component were determined at issuance of the bond.

The convertible bond recognised in the balance sheet is calculated as follows:

	2013	2012
Face value of convertible bond issued on 2 January 2013	50,000	–
Equity component (note 29)	(7,761)	–
Liability component on initial recognition at 2 January 2013	42,239	–
Interest expense (note 11)	3,083	–
Interest paid	(2,500)	–
Liability component at 31 December 2013	42,822	–

12AppxBEx4 *(appears beside Equity component row)*

IFRS13p93(b),
(d), IFRS13p97
The fair value of the liability component of the convertible bond at 31 December 2013 amounted to C42,617. The fair value is calculated using cash flows discounted at a rate based on the borrowings rate of 7.5% and are within level 2 of the fair value hierarchy.

(c) Redeemable preference shares

32p15,
32p18(a)
The group issued 30 million cumulative redeemable preference shares with a par value of C1 per share on 4 January 2012. The shares are mandatorily redeemable at their par value on 4 January 2016, and pay dividends at 6.5% annually.

10p21
On 1 February 2014, the group issued C6,777 6.5% US dollar bonds to finance its expansion programme and working capital requirements in the US. The bonds are repayable on 31 December 2017.

(d) Finance lease liabilities

Lease liabilities are effectively secured as the rights to the leased asset revert to the lessor in the event of default.

	2013	2012
Gross finance lease liabilities– minimum lease payments:		
No later than 1 year	2,749	3,203
Later than 1 year and no later than 5 years	6,292	7,160
Later than 5 years	2,063	2,891
	11,104	13,254
Future finance charges on finance lease liabilities	(2,106)	(2,656)
Present value of finance lease liabilities	8,998	10,598

17p31(b) *(appears beside Gross finance lease liabilities row)*

[1] This amount is not in C thousands.

Notes to the consolidated financial statements

(All amounts in C thousands unless otherwise stated)

17p31(b) The present value of finance lease liabilities is as follows:

	2013	2012
No later than 1 year	2,192	2,588
Later than 1 year and no later than 5 years	4,900	5,287
Later than 5 years	1,906	2,723
	8,998	10,598

32 Deferred income tax

The analysis of deferred tax assets and deferred tax liabilities is as follows:

	2013	2012 Restated
Deferred tax assets:		
– Deferred tax assets to be recovered after more than 12 months	(2,899)	(3,319)
– Deferred tax asset to be recovered within 12 months	(647)	(64)
	(3,546)	(3,383)
Deferred tax liabilities:		
– Deferred tax liability to be recovered after more than 12 months	10,743	8,016
– Deferred tax liability to be recovered within 12 months	1,627	1,037
	12,370	9,053
Deferred tax liabilities (net)	8,824	5,670

1p61 appears to the left of "Deferred tax assets:" row.

The gross movement on the deferred income tax account is as follows:

	2013	2012 Restated
At 1 January	5,670	3,047
Exchange differences	(2,003)	(154)
Acquisition of subsidiary (note 39)	1,953	–
Income statement charge (note 13)	379	2,635
Tax charge /(credit) relating to components of other comprehensive income (note 13)	527	162
Tax charged/(credited) directly to equity (note 13)	2,298	(20)
At 31 December	8,824	5,670

(All amounts in C thousands unless otherwise stated)

12p81(g)(i)(ii) The movement in deferred income tax assets and liabilities during the year, without taking into consideration the offsetting of balances within the same tax jurisdiction, is as follows:

Deferred tax liabilities	Accelerated tax depreciation	Fair value gains	Convertible bond	Other	Total
At 1 January 2012 (Restated)	6,412	413	–	284	7,109
12p81(g)(ii) Charged/(credited) to the income statement	1,786	–	–	799	2,585
12p81(e) Charged/(credited) to other comprehensive income	–	435	–	–	435
Exchange difference	(100)	–	–	(54)	(154)
12p81(g)(i) At 31 December 2012 (Restated)	8,098	848	–	1,029	9,975
12p81(g)(ii) Charged/(credited) to the income statement	425	–	(193)	388	620
12p81(e) Charged/(credited)/charged to other comprehensive income	–	448	–	43	491
12p81(a) Charged directly to equity	–	–	2,328	–	2,328
Acquisition of subsidiary	553	1,125	–	275	1,953
Exchange difference	(333)	(600)	–	(350)	(1,283)
12p81(g)(i) **At 31 December 2013**	**8,743**	**1,821**	**2,135**	**1,385**	**14,084**

Deferred tax assets	Retirement benefit obligation	Provisions	Impairment losses	Tax losses	Other	Total
At 1 January 2012 (Restated)	(428)	(997)	(732)	(1,532)	(373)	(4,062)
12p81(g)(ii) Charged/(credited) to the income statement	–	181	–	–	(131)	50
12p81(e) Charged/(credited) to other comprehensive income	(273)	–	–	–	–	(273)
12p81(a) Charged/(credited) directly to equity	–	–	–	–	(20)	(20)
Exchange difference	–	–	–	–	–	–
12p81(g)(i) At 31 December 2012 (Restated)	(701)	(816)	(732)	(1,532)	(524)	(4,305)
12p81(g)(ii) Charged/(credited) to the income statement	–	(538)	(322)	750	(131)	(241)
12p81(e) Charged/(credited) to other comprehensive income	36	–	–	–	–	36
12p81(a) Charged/(credited) directly to equity	–	–	–	–	(30)	(30)
Exchange difference	(150)	(280)	(210)	–	(80)	(720)
12p81(g)(i) **At 31 December 2012**	**(815)**	**(1,634)**	**(1,264)**	**(782)**	**(765)**	**(5,260)**

12p81(e) Deferred income tax assets are recognised for tax loss carry-forwards to the extent that the realisation of the related tax benefit through future taxable profits is probable. The group did not recognise deferred income tax assets of C333 (2012: C1,588) in respect of losses amounting to C1,000 (2012: C5,294) that can be carried forward against future taxable income. Losses amounting to C900 (2012: C5,294) and C100 (2012: nil) expire in 2014 and 2015 respectively.

Notes to the consolidated financial statements

(All amounts in C thousands unless otherwise stated)

12p81(f)   Deferred income tax liabilities of C3,141 (2012: C2,016) have not been recognised for the withholding tax and other taxes that would be payable on the unremitted earnings of certain subsidiaries. Such amounts are permanently reinvested. Unremitted earnings totalled C30,671 at 31 December 2013 (2012: C23,294).

33 Post-employment benefits

The table below outlines where the group's post-employment amounts and activity are included in the financial statements.

	2013	2012 Restated
Balance sheet obligations for:		
– Defined pension benefits	3,684	1,900
– Post-employment medical benefits	1,432	711
Liability in the balance sheet	5,116	2,611
Income statement charge included in operating profit for[1]:		
– Defined pension benefits	948	561
– Post-employment medical benefits	184	119
	1,132	680
Remeasurements for:		
– Defined pension benefits	(84)	717
– Post-employment medical benefits	(35)	193
	(119)	910

33(a) Defined benefit pension plans

DV, 19Rp136, 19Rp138 19Rp139   The group operates defined benefit pension plans in the UK and US under broadly similar regulatory frameworks. All of the plans are final salary pension plans, which provide benefits to members in the form of a guaranteed level of pension payable for life. The level of benefits provided depends on members' length of service and their salary in the final years leading up to retirement. In the UK plans, pensions in payment are generally updated in line with the retail price index, whereas in the US plans, pensions generally do not receive inflationary increases once in payment. With the exception of this inflationary risk in the UK, the plans face broadly similar risks, as described below. The majority of benefit payments are from trustee-administered funds; however, there are also a number of unfunded plans where the company meets the benefit payment obligation as it falls due. Plan assets held in trusts are governed by local regulations and practice in each country, as is the nature of the relationship between the group and the trustees (or equivalent) and their composition. Responsibility for governance of the plans – including investment decisions and contribution schedules – lies jointly with the company and the board of trustees. The board of trustees must be composed of representatives of the company and plan participants in accordance with the plan's regulations.

[1] The income statement charge included within operating profit includes current service cost, interest cost, past service costs and gains and losses on settlement and curtailment.

(All amounts in C thousands unless otherwise stated)

19Rp140(a)	The amounts recognised in the balance sheet are determined as follows:		
		2013	2012 Restated
	Present value of funded obligations	**6,155**	2,943
	Fair value of plan assets	**(5,211)**	(2,797)
	Deficit of funded plans	**944**	146
	Present value of unfunded obligations	**2,426**	1,549
	Total deficit of defined benefit pension plans	**3,370**	1,695
	Impact of minimum funding requirement/asset ceiling	**314**	205
	Liability in the balance sheet	**3,684**	1,900

19Rp140(a),
141(a-h)

The movement in the defined benefit obligation over the year is as follows:

	Present value of obligation	Fair value of plan assets	Total	Impact of minimum funding requirement/ asset ceiling	Total
At 1 January 2012 (Restated)	3,479	(2,264)	1,215	120	1,335
Current service cost	498	–	498	–	498
Interest expense/(income)	214	(156)	58	5	63
	712	(156)	556	5	561
Remeasurements:					
– Return on plan assets, excluding amounts included in interest expense/(income)	–	(85)	(85)	–	(85)
– (Gain)/loss from change in demographic assumptions	20	–	20	–	20
– (Gain)/loss from change in financial assumptions	61	–	61	–	61
– Experience (gains)/losses	641	–	641	–	641
– Change in asset ceiling, excluding amounts included in interest expense	0	–	–	80	80
	722	(85)	637	80	717
Exchange differences	(324)	22	(302)	–	(302)
Contributions:					
– Employers	–	(411)	(411)	–	(411)
– Plan participants	30	(30)	–	–	–
Payments from plans:					
– Benefit payments	(127)	127	–	–	–
At 31 December 2012 (Restated)	4,492	(2,797)	1,695	205	1,900

Notes to the consolidated financial statements

(All amounts in C thousands unless otherwise stated)

	Present value of obligation	Fair value of plan assets	Total	Impact of minimum funding requirement/ asset ceiling	Total
At 1 January 2013	4,492	(2,797)	1,695	205	1,900
Current service cost	751	–	751	–	751
Interest expense/(income)	431	(308)	123	9	132
Past service cost and gains and losses on settlements	65	–	65	–	65
	1,247	(308)	939	9	948
Remeasurements:					
– Return on plan assets, excluding amounts included in interest expense/(income)	–	(187)	(187)	–	(187)
– (Gain)/loss from change in demographic assumptions	32	–	32	–	32
– (Gain)/loss from change in financial assumptions	121	–	121	–	121
– Experience (gains)/losses	(150)	–	(150)	–	(150)
– Change in asset ceiling, excluding amounts included in interest expense	–	–	–	100	100
	3	(187)	(184)	100	(84)
Exchange differences	(61)	(25)	(86)	–	(86)
Contributions:					
– Employers	–	(908)	(908)	–	(908)
– Plan participants	55	(55)	–	–	–
Payments from plans:					
– Benefit payments	(566)	566	–	–	–
– Settlements	(280)	280	–	–	–
Acquired in a business combination	3,691	(1,777)	1,914	–	1,914
At 31 December 2013	**8,581**	**(5,211)**	**3,370**	**314**	**3,684**

19Rp141   One of our US plans has a surplus that is not recognised on the basis that future economic benefits are not available to the entity in the form of a reduction in future contributions or a cash refund.

19Rp139 (c)   In connection with the closure of a factory, a curtailment loss was incurred and a settlement arrangement agreed with the plan trustees, effective December 30, 2012, which settled all retirement benefit plan obligations relating to the employees of that factory.

(All amounts in C thousands unless otherwise stated)

DV   The defined benefit obligation and plan assets are composed by country as follows:

| | 2013 | | | 2012 Restated | | |
	UK	US	Total	UK	US	Total
Present value of obligation	4,366	4,215	8,581	3,442	1,050	4,492
Fair value of plan assets	(3,109)	(2,102)	(5,211)	(2,403)	(394)	(2,797)
	1,257	2,113	3,370	1,039	656	1,695
Impact of minimum funding requirement/asset ceiling	–	314	314	–	205	205
Total	1,257	2,427	3,684	1,039	861	1,900

As at the last valuation date, the present value of the defined benefit obligation was comprised of approximately C3,120 relating to active employees, C3,900 relating to deferred members and C1,560 relating to members in retirement.

19Rp144   The significant actuarial assumptions were as follows:

| | 2013 | | 2012 | |
	UK	US	UK	US
Discount rate	5.1%	5.2%	5.5%	5.6%
Inflation	3.0%	4.0%	3.5%	4.2%
Salary growth rate	4.0%	4.5%	4.5%	4.0%
Pension growth rate	3.0%	2.8%	3.1%	2.7%

Assumptions regarding future mortality are set based on actuarial advice in accordance with published statistics and experience in each territory. These assumptions translate into an average life expectancy in years for a pensioner retiring at age 65:

| | 2013 | | 2012 | |
	UK	US	UK	US
Retiring at the end of the reporting period:				
– Male	22	20	22	20
– Female	25	24	25	24
Retiring 20 years after the end of the reporting period				
– Male	24	23	24	23
– Female	27	26	27	26

Notes to the consolidated financial statements

(All amounts in C thousands unless otherwise stated)

19Rp145(a) The sensitivity of the defined benefit obligation to changes in the weighted principal assumptions is:

		Impact on defined benefit obligation	
	Change in assumption	Increase in assumption	Decrease in assumption
Discount rate	0.50%	Decrease by 8.2%	Increase by 9.0%
Salary growth rate	0.50%	Increase by 1.8%	Decrease by 1.7%
Pension growth rate	0.25%	Increase by 4.7%	Decrease by 4.4%
		Increase by 1 year in assumption	Decrease by 1 year in assumption
Life expectancy		Increase by 2.8%	Decrease by 2.9%

19Rp145(b) The above sensitivity analyses are based on a change in an assumption while holding all other assumptions constant. In practice, this is unlikely to occur, and changes in some of the assumptions may be correlated. When calculating the sensitivity of the defined benefit obligation to significant actuarial assumptions the same method (present value of the defined benefit obligation calculated with the projected unit credit method at the end of the reporting period) has been applied as when calculating the pension liability recognised within the statement of financial position.

19Rp145(c) The methods and types of assumptions used in preparing the sensitivity analysis did not change compared to the previous period.

33(b) Post-employment medical benefits

DV, 19Rp144 The group operates a number of post-employment medical benefit schemes, principally in the US. The majority of these plans are unfunded. The method of accounting, significant assumptions and the frequency of valuations are similar to those used for defined benefit pension schemes set out above with the addition of actuarial assumptions relating to the long-term increase in healthcare costs of 8.0% a year (2012:7.6%) and claim rates of 6% (2012: 5.2%).

19Rp140(a) The amounts recognised in the balance sheet are determined as follows:

	2013	2012 Restated
Present value of funded obligations	727	350
Fair value of plan assets	(605)	(294)
Deficit of the funded plans	122	56
Present value of unfunded obligations	1,310	655
Liability in the balance sheet	**1,432**	711

(All amounts in C thousands unless otherwise stated)

19Rp140(a),
141(a-h)

The movement in the defined benefit liability over the year is as follows:

	Present value of obligation	Fair value of plan assets	Total
At 1 January 2012 (Restated)	708	(207)	501
Current service cost	107	–	107
Interest expense/(income)	25	(13)	12
	132	(13)	119
Remeasurements:			
– Return on plan assets, excluding amounts included in interest expense/(income)	–	(11)	(11)
– (Gain)/loss from change in demographic assumptions	3	–	3
– (Gain)/loss from change in financial assumptions	7	–	7
– Experience (gains)/losses	194	–	194
	204	(11)	193
Exchange differences	(31)	2	(29)
Contributions/premiums paid:			
– Employers	–	(73)	(73)
Payments from plans:			
– Benefit payments	(8)	8	–
At 31 December 2012 (Restated)	1,005	(294)	711
At 1 January 2013	1,005	(294)	711
Current service cost	153	–	153
Interest expense/(income)	49	(18)	31
	202	(18)	184
Remeasurements:			
– Return on plan assets, excluding amounts included in interest expense/(income)	–	(33)	(33)
– (Gain)/loss from change in demographic assumptions	4	–	4
– (Gain)/loss from change in financial assumptions	10	–	10
– Experience (gains)/losses	(16)	–	(16)
	(2)	(33)	(35)
Exchange differences	37	(5)	32
Contributions/premiums paid:			
– Employers	–	(185)	(185)
Payments from plans:			
– Benefit payments	(7)	7	–
Acquired in a business combination (note 39)	802	(77)	725
At 31 December 2013	2,037	(605)	1,432

(All amounts in C thousands unless otherwise stated)

33(c) Post-employment benefits (pension and medical)

19Rp142 Plan assets are comprised as follows:

	2013				2012			
	Quoted	Unquoted	**Total**	**%**	Quoted	Unquoted	Total	%
Equity instruments			**1,824**	**31%**			1,216	39%
Information technology	502	–	502		994	–	994	
Energy	557	–	557		–	–	–	
Manufacturing	746	–	746		194	–	194	
Other	–	19	19		–	28	28	
Debt instruments			**2,161**	**37%**			571	18%
Government	916	–	916		321	–	321	
Corporate bonds (Investment grade)	900	–	900		99	–	99	
Corporate bonds (Non-investment grade)	68	277	345		41	110	151	
Property			**1,047**	**18%**			943	31%
in US	–	800	800		–	697	697	
in UK	–	247	247		–	246	246	
Qualifying insurance policies	–	496	**496**	**9%**	–	190	190	6%
Cash and cash equivalents	177	–	**177**	**3%**	94	–	94	3%
Investment funds	111	–	**111**	**2%**	77	–	77	2%
Total	**3,977**	**1,839**	**5,816**	**100%**	**1,820**	**1,271**	**3,091**	**100%**

19Rp143 Pension and medical plan assets include the company's ordinary shares with a fair value of C136 (2012: C126) and US real estate occupied by the group with a fair value of C612 (2012: C609).

19Rp139(b) Through its defined benefit pension plans and post-employment medical plans, the group is exposed to a number of risks, the most significant of which are detailed below:

Asset volatility   The plan liabilities are calculated using a discount rate set with reference to corporate bond yields; if plan assets underperform this yield, this will create a deficit. Both the UK and US plans hold a significant proportion of equities, which are expected to outperform corporate bonds in the long-term while providing volatility and risk in the short-term.

As the plans mature, the group intends to reduce the level of investment risk by investing more in assets that better match the liabilities. The first stage of this process was completed in FY12 with the sale of a number of equity holdings and purchase of a mixture of government and corporate bonds. The government bonds represent investments in UK and US government securities only. The corporate bonds are global securities with an emphasis on the UK and US.

However, the group believes that due to the long-term nature of the plan liabilities and the strength of the supporting group, a level of continuing equity investment is an appropriate element of the group's long term strategy to manage the plans efficiently. See below for more details on the group's asset-liability matching strategy.

(All amounts in C thousands unless otherwise stated)

	Changes in bond yields	A decrease in corporate bond yields will increase plan liabilities, although this will be partially offset by an increase in the value of the plans' bond holdings.
	Inflation risk	The some of the group pension obligations are linked to inflation, and higher inflation will lead to higher liabilities (although, in most cases, caps on the level of inflationary increases are in place to protect the plan against extreme inflation). The majority of the plan's assets are either unaffected by (fixed interest bonds) or loosely correlated with (equities) inflation, meaning that an increase in inflation will also increase the deficit.
		In the US plans, the pensions in payment are not linked to inflation, so this is a less material risk.
	Life expectancy	The majority of the plans' obligations are to provide benefits for the life of the member, so increases in life expectancy will result in an increase in the plans' liabilities. This is particularly significant in the UK plan, where inflationary increases result in higher sensitivity to changes in life expectancy.

19Rp146   In case of the funded plans, the group ensures that the investment positions are managed within an asset-liability matching (ALM) framework that has been developed to achieve long-term investments that are in line with the obligations under the pension schemes. Within this framework, the Group's ALM objective is to match assets to the pension obligations by investing in long-term fixed interest securities with maturites that match the benefit payments as they fall due and in the appropriate currency. The company actively monitors how the duration and the expected yield of the investments are matching the expected cash outflows arising from the pension obligations. The group has not changed the processes used to manage its risks from previous periods. The group does not use derivatives to manage its risk. Investments are well diversified, such that the failure of any single investment would not have a material impact on the overall level of assets. A large portion of assets in 2013 consists of equities and bonds, although the group also invests in property, bonds, cash and investment (hedge) funds. The group believes that equities offer the best returns over the long term with an acceptable level of risk. The majority of equities are in a globally diversified portfolio of international blue chip entities, with a target of 60% of equities held in the UK and Europe, 30% in the US and the remainder in emerging markets.

19Rp147(a)   The group has agreed that it will aim to eliminate the pension plan deficit over the next nine years. Funding levels are monitored on an annual basis and the current agreed contribution rate is 14% of pensionable salaries in the UK and 12% in the US. The next triennial valuation is due to be completed as at 31 December 2014. The group considers that the contribution rates set at the last valuation date are sufficient to eliminate the deficit over the agreed period and that regular contributions, which are based on service costs, will not increase significantly.

19Rp147(b)   Expected contributions to post-employment benefit plans for the year ending 31 December 2014 are C1,150.

19Rp147(c)   The weighted average duration of the defined benefit obligation is 25.2 years.

(All amounts in C thousands unless otherwise stated)

19Rp147(c)	Expected maturity analysis of undiscounted pension and post-employment medical benefits:					
	At 31 December 2013	**Less than a year**	**Between 1-2 years**	**Between 2-5 years**	**Over 5 years**	**Total**
	Pension benefits	628	927	2,004	21,947	25,506
	Post-employment medical benefits	127	174	714	4,975	5,990
	Total	**755**	**1,101**	**2,718**	**26,922**	**31,496**

34 Dividends per share

1p107,
1p137(a),
10p12

The dividends paid in 2013 and 2012 were C10,102 (C0.48 per share) and C15,736 (C0.78 per share) respectively. A dividend in respect of the year ended 31 December 2013 of C0.51 per share, amounting to a total dividend of C12,945, is to be proposed at the annual general meeting on 30 April 2014. These financial statements do not reflect this dividend payable.

35 Provisions for other liabilities and charges

1p78(d)		Environ-mental restoration	Restruc-turing	Legal claims	Profit-sharing and bonuses	Contingent liability arising on a business combination	Total
37p84(a)	At 1 January 2013 (restated)	842	–	828	1,000	–	2,670
	Charged/(credited) to the income statement:						
37p84(b)	– Additional provisions	316	1,986	2,405	500	–	5,207
	– On acquisition of ABC Group	–	–	–	–	1,000	1,000
37p84(d)	– Unused amounts reversed	(15)	–	(15)	(10)	–	(40)
37p84(e)	– Unwinding of discount	40	–	–	–	4	44
37p84(c)	Used during year	(233)	(886)	(3,059)	(990)	–	(5,168)
	Exchange differences	(7)	–	(68)	–	–	(75)
IFRS5p38	Transferred to disposal group classified as held for sale	(96)	–	–	–	–	(96)
37p84(a)	**At 31 December 2013**	**847**	**1,100**	**91**	**500**	**1,004**	**3,542**

Analysis of total provisions:

		2013	2012 Restated
1p69	Non-current	316	274
1p69	Current	3,226	2,396
	Total	**3,542**	**2,670**

(All amounts in C thousands unless otherwise stated)

(a) Environmental restoration

37p85(a(-(c) The group uses various chemicals in working with leather. A provision is recognised for the present value of costs to be incurred for the restoration of the manufacturing sites. It is expected that C531 will be used during 2014 and C316 during 2015. Total expected costs to be incurred are C880 (2012: C760).

DV The provision transferred to the disposal group classified as held for sale amounts to C96 and relates to an environmental restoration provision for Shoes Limited (part of the UK wholesale segment). See note 25 for further details regarding the disposal group held for sale.

(b) Restructuring

37p85(a)-(c) The reduction of the volumes assigned to manufacturing operations in Step-land (a subsidiary) will result in the reduction of a total of 155 jobs at two factories. An agreement was reached with the local union representatives, which specifies the number of staff involved and the voluntary redundancy compensation package offered by the group, as well as amounts payable to those made redundant, before the financial year-end. The estimated staff restructuring costs to be incurred are C799 at 31 December 2013 (note 10a). Other direct costs attributable to the restructuring, including lease termination, are C1,187. These costs were fully provided for in 2013. The provision of C1,100 at 31 December 2013 is expected to be fully utilised during the first half of 2014.

36p130 A goodwill impairment charge of C4,650 was recognised in the cash-generating unit relating to Step-land as a result of this restructuring (note 17).

(c) Legal claims

37p85(a)-(c) The amounts represent a provision for certain legal claims brought against the group by customers of the US wholesale segment. The provision charge is recognised in profit or loss within 'administrative expenses'. The balance at 31 December 2013 is expected to be utilised in the first half of 2014. In the directors' opinion, after taking appropriate legal advice, the outcome of these legal claims will not give rise to any significant loss beyond the amounts provided at 31 December 2013.

(d) Profit-sharing and bonuses

19p8(c),10, DV, The provision for profit-sharing and bonuses is payable within three months of the
37p85(a)-(c) finalisation of the audited financial statements.

(e) Recognised contingent liability

19p8(c),10, DV, A contingent liability of C1,000 has been recognised on the acquisition of ABC Group
37p85(a)-(c) for a pending lawsuit in which the entity is a defendant. The claim has arisen from a customer alleging defects on products supplied to them. It is expected that the courts will have reached a decision on this case by the end of 2014. The potential undiscounted amount of all future payments that the group could be required to make if there was an adverse decision related to the lawsuit is estimated to be between C500 and C1,500. As of 31 December 2013, there has been no change in the amount recognised (except for the unwinding of the discount of C4) for the liability at 31 March 2013, as there has been no change in the probability of the outcome of the lawsuit.

Notes to the consolidated financial statements

(All amounts in C thousands unless otherwise stated)

IFRS3B64(g) The selling shareholders of ABC Group have contractually agreed to indemnify IFRS GAAP plc for the claim that may become payable in respect of the above-mentioned lawsuit. An indemnification asset of C1,000, equivalent to the fair value of the indemnified liability, has been recognised by the group. The indemnification asset is deducted from consideration transferred for the business combination. As is the case with the indemnified liability, there has been no change in the amount recognised for the indemnification asset as at 31 December 2013, as there has been no change in the range of outcomes or assumptions used to develop the estimate of the liability.

36 Cash generated from operations

	2013	2012 Restated
7p18(b), 7p20 Profit before income tax including discontinued operations	**49,100**	25,837
Adjustments for:		
– Depreciation (note 16)	**17,754**	9,662
– Amortisation (note 17)	**800**	565
– Goodwill impairment charge (note 17)	**4,650**	–
– (Profit)/loss on disposal of property, plant and equipment	**(17)**	8
– Share-based payment	**690**	822
– Post-employment benefits	**39**	196
– Fair value gains on derivative financial instruments (note 8)	**(86)**	(88)
– Fair value (gains)/losses on financial assets at fair value through profit or loss (note 8)	**(85)**	238
– Dividend income on available-for-sale financial assets (note 7)	**(1,100)**	(883)
– Dividend income on financial assets at fair value through profit or loss (note 7)	**(800)**	(310)
– Provision for restructuring cost	**1,100**	–
– Inventory write-down (note 6)	**3,117**	–
– Finance costs – net (note 11)	**6,443**	10,588
– Share of loss/(profit) from joint ventures and associates (note 12)	**(1,682)**	(1,022)
– Foreign exchange losses/(gains) on operating activities (note 8)	**277**	(200)
Gains on revaluation of available-for-sale investments (note 7)	**(850)**	–
Changes in working capital (excluding the effects of acquisition and exchange differences on consolidation):		
– Inventories	**(3,073)**	(966)
– Trade and other receivables	**1,203**	(2,429)
– Financial assets at fair value through profit or loss	**(3,883)**	(858)
– Trade and other payables	**1,154**	543
Cash generated from operations	**74,751**	41,703

In the statement of cash flows, proceeds from sale of property, plant and equipment comprise:

	2013	2012
Net book amount (note 16)	**6,337**	2,987
Profit/(loss) on disposal of property, plant and equipment	**17**	(8)
Proceeds from disposal of property, plant and equipment	**6,354**	2,979

7p43 *Non-cash transactions*

The principal non-cash transaction is the issue of shares as consideration for the acquisition discussed in note 39.

(All amounts in C thousands unless otherwise stated)

37 Contingencies

37p86   Since 2011, the Group has been defending an action brought by an environment agency in Europe. The group has disclaimed the liability.

No provision in relation to this claim has been recognised in these consolidated financial statements, as legal advice indicates that it is not probable that a significant liability will arise. Further claims for which provisions have been made are reflected in note 35.

38 Commitments

(a) Capital commitments

Capital expenditure contracted for at the end of the reporting period but not yet incurred is as follows:

	2013	2012 Restated
16p74(c) Property, plant and equipment	3,593	3,667
38p122(e) Intangible assets	460	474
Total	**4,053**	4,141

(b) Operating lease commitments – group company as lessee

17p35(d)   The group leases various retail outlets, offices and warehouses under non-cancellable operating lease agreements. The lease terms are between 5 and 10 years, and the majority of lease agreements are renewable at the end of the lease period at market rate.

17p35(d)   The group also leases various plant and machinery under cancellable operating lease agreements. The group is required to give a six-month notice for the termination of these agreements. The lease expenditure charged to the income statement during the year is disclosed in note 9.

17p35(a)   The future aggregate minimum lease payments under non-cancellable operating leases are as follows:

	2013	2012 Restated
No later than 1 year	11,664	10,604
Later than 1 year and no later than 5 years	45,651	45,651
Later than 5 years	15,710	27,374
Total	**73,025**	83,629

Notes to the consolidated financial statements

(All amounts in C thousands unless otherwise stated)

39 Business combinations

IFRS3B64(a)(d) On 30 June 2012, the group acquired 15% of the share capital of ABC Group for C1,150. On 1 March 2013, the group acquired a further 56.73% of the share capital and obtained control of ABC Group, a shoe and leather goods retailer operating in the US and a wholesaler operating in most western European countries.

IFRS3B64(e) As a result of the acquisition, the group is expected to increase its presence in these markets. It also expects to reduce costs through economies of scale. The goodwill of C4,501 arising from the acquisition is attributable to acquired customer base and economies of scale expected from combining the operations of the group and ABC Group. None of the goodwill recognised is expected to be deductible for income tax purposes.

IFRS3B64(k) The following table summarises the consideration paid for ABC group, the fair value of assets acquired, liabilities assumed and the non-controlling interest at the acquisition date.

Consideration at 1 March 2013

IFRS3B64(f)(i), IFRS3B64(f)(iv)	Cash	4,050
IFRS3B64(f)(iii)	Equity instruments (3.55m ordinary shares)	10,000
IFRS3B64(g)(i)	Contingent consideration	1,000
IFRS3B64(f)	**Total consideration transferred**	**15,050**
	Indemnification asset	(1,000)
IFRS3B64(p)(i)	Fair value of equity interest in ABC Group held before the business combination	2,000
	Total consideration	**16,050**

IFRS3B64(i)	**Recognised amounts of identifiable assets acquired and liabilities assumed**	
	Cash and cash equivalents	300
	Property, plant and equipment (note 16)	67,784
	Trademarks (included in intangibles) (note 17)	2,500
	Licences (included in intangibles) (note 17)	1,500
	Available-for-sale financial assets (note 19)	473
	Inventories	459
	Trade and other receivables	585
	Trade and other payables	(11,409)
	Retirement benefit obligations:	
	– Pensions (note 33)	(1,914)
	– Other post-retirement obligations (note 33)	(725)
	Borrowings	(40,509)
	Contingent liability	(1,000)
	Deferred tax liabilities (note 32)	(1,953)
	Total identifiable net assets	**16,091**
IFRS3B64(o)(i)	**Non-controlling interest**	(4,542)
	Goodwill	4,501
	Total	**16,050**

(All amounts in C thousands unless otherwise stated)

IFRS3B64(m)	Acquisition-related costs of C200 have been charged to administrative expenses in the consolidated income statement for the year ended 31 December 2013.
IFRS3B 64 (f)(iv), IFRSB64(m)	The fair value of the 3,550 thousand ordinary shares issued as part of the consideration paid for ABC Group (C10,050) was based on the published share price on 1 March 2013. Issuance costs totalling C50 have been netted against the deemed proceeds.
IFRS3B 64(f)(iii), IFRS3B64(g), IFRS3B67(b)	The contingent consideration arrangement requires the group to pay, in cash, to the former owners of ABC Group, 10% of the average profit of ABC Group for three years from 2013 – 2015, in excess of C7,500, up to a maximum undiscounted amount of C2,500.
	The potential undiscounted amount of all future payments that the group could be required to make under this arrangement is between C0 and C2,500.
	The fair value of the contingent consideration arrangement of C1,000 was estimated by applying the income approach. The fair value estimates are based on a discount rate of 8% and assumed probability-adjusted profit in ABC Group of C10,000 to C20,000. This is a level 3 fair value measurement.
	As of 31 December 2013, there was an increase of C500 recognised in the income statement for the contingent consideration arrangement, as the assumed probability-adjusted profit in ABC Group was recalculated to be approximately C20,000-30,000.
IFRS3B64(h)	The fair value of trade and other receivables is C585 and includes trade receivables with a fair value of C510. The gross contractual amount for trade receivables due is C960, of which C450 is expected to be uncollectible.
IFRS3B67(a)	The fair value of the acquired identifiable intangible assets of C4,000 (including trademarks and licences) is provisional pending receipt of the final valuations for those assets.
IFRS3B64(j), IFRS3B67(c), 37p84, 37p85	A contingent liability of C1,000 has been recognised for a pending lawsuit in which ABC Group is a defendant. The claim has arisen from a customer alleging defects on products supplied to them. It is expected that the courts will have reached a decision on this case by the end of 2014. The potential undiscounted amount of all future payments that the group could be required to make if there was an adverse decision related to the lawsuit is estimated to be between C500 and C1,500. As of 31 December 2013, there has been no change in the amount recognised (except for unwinding of the discount C4) for the liability at 1 March 2013, as there has been no change in the range of outcomes or assumptions used to develop the estimates.
IFRS3B64(g), IFRS3p57	The selling shareholders of ABC Group have contractually agreed to indemnify IFRS GAAP plc for the claim that may become payable in respect of the above-mentioned lawsuit. An indemnification asset of C1,000, equivalent to the fair value of the indemnified liability, has been recognised by the group. The indemnification asset is deducted from consideration transferred for the business combination. As is the case with the indemnified liability, there has been no change in the amount recognised for the indemnification asset as at 31 December 2013, as there has been no change in the range of outcomes or assumptions used to develop the estimate of the liability.
IFRS3B64(o)	The fair value of the non-controlling interest in ABC Group, an unlisted company, was estimated by using the purchase price paid for acquisition of 55% stake in ABC group. This purchase price was adjusted for the lack of control and lack of

(All amounts in C thousands unless otherwise stated)

marketability that market participants would consider when estimating the fair value of the non-controlling interest in ABC Group.

IFRS3B64(p)(ii) The group recognised a gain of C850 as a result of measuring at fair value its 15% equity interest in ABC Group held before the business combination. The gain is included in other income in the group's statement of comprehensive income for the year ended 31 December 2013.

IFRS3B64(q)(i) The revenue included in the consolidated statement of comprehensive income since 1 March 2013 contributed by ABC Group was C44,709. ABC Group also contributed profit of C12,762 over the same period.

IFRS3B64(q)(ii) Had ABC Group been consolidated from 1 January 2013, the consolidated statement of income would show pro-forma revenue[1] of C220,345 and profit of C35,565.

40 Transactions with non-controlling interests

(a) Acquisition of additional interest in a subsidiary

IFRS12p18 On 21 April 2013, the company acquired the remaining 5% of the issued shares of XYZ group for a purchase consideration of C1,100. The group now holds 100% of the equity share capital of XYZ group. The carrying amount of the non-controlling interests in XYZ group on the date of acquisition was C300. The group derecognised non-controlling interests of C300 and recorded a decrease in equity attributable to owners of the parent of C800. The effect of changes in the ownership interest of XYZ group on the equity attributable to owners of the company during the year is summarised as follows:

	2013	2012
Carrying amount of non-controlling interests acquired	300	–
Consideration paid to non-controlling interests	(1,100)	–
Excess of consideration paid recognised in parent's equity	(800)	–

(b) Disposal of interest in a subsidiary without loss of control

IFRS12p18 On 5 September 2013, the company disposed of a 10% interest out of the 80% interest held in Red Limited at a consideration of C1,100. The carrying amount of the non-controlling interests in Red Limited on the date of disposal was C2,000 (representing 20% interest). This resulted in an increase in non-controlling interests of C1,000 and an increase in equity attributable to owners of the parent of C100. The effect of changes in the ownership interest of Red Limited on the equity attributable to owners of the company during the year is summarised as follows:

	31 December 2013	31 December 2012
Carrying amount of non-controlling interests disposed of	(1,000)	–
Consideration received from non-controlling interests	1,100	–
Increase in parent's equity	100	–

There were no transactions with non-controlling interests in 2012.

---

[1] The information on combined revenue and profit does not represent actual results for the year and is therefore labelled as pro-forma.

(All amounts in C thousands unless otherwise stated)

IFRS12p18 **(c) Effects of transactions with non-controlling interests on the equity attributable to owners of the parent for the year ended 31 December 2013**

	31 December 2013
Changes in equity attributable to shareholders of the company arising from:	
– Acquisition of additional interests in a subsidiary	(800)
– Disposal of interests in a subsidiary without loss of control	100
Net effect on parent's equity	**(700)**

41 Related parties

1p138(c), 24p13 The group is controlled by M Limited (incorporated in the UK), which owns 57% of the company's shares. The remaining 43% of the shares are widely held. The group's ultimate parent is G Limited (incorporated in the UK). The group's ultimate controlling party is Mr Wong.

24p18, p19, p24 The following transactions were carried out with related parties:

24p18(a) *(a) Sales of goods and services*

	2013	2012
Sale of goods:		
– Associates	1,002	204
– Associates of G Limited	121	87
Sales of services:		
– Ultimate parent (legal and administration services)	67	127
– Close family members of the ultimate controlling party (design services)	100	104
Total	**1,290**	**522**

Goods are sold based on the price lists in force and terms that would be available to third parties[1]. Sales of services are negotiated with related parties on a cost-plus basis, allowing a margin ranging from 15% to 30% (2012: 10% to 18%).

(b) Purchases of goods and services

24p18(a)

	2013	2012
Purchase of goods:		
– Associates	3,054	3,058
Purchase of services:		
– Entity controlled by key management personnel	83	70
– Immediate parent (management services)	295	268
Total	**3,432**	**3,396**

[1] Management should disclose that related-party transactions were made on an arm's length basis only when such terms can be substantiated (24p23).

Notes to the consolidated financial statements

(All amounts in C thousands unless otherwise stated)

24p23 Goods and services are bought from associates and an entity controlled by key management personnel on normal commercial terms and conditions. The entity controlled by key management personnel is a firm belonging to Mr Chamois, a non-executive director of the company. Management services are bought from the immediate parent on a cost-plus basis, allowing a margin ranging from 15% to 30% (2012: 10% to 24%).

24p17 *(c) Key management compensation*

Key management includes directors (executive and non-executive), members of the Executive Committee, the Company Secretary and the Head of Internal Audit. The compensation paid or payable to key management for employee services is shown below:

		2013	2012
24p17(a)	Salaries and other short-term employee benefits	2,200	1890
24p17(d)	Termination benefits	1,600	–
24p17(b)	Post-employment benefits	123	85
24p17(c)	Other long-term benefits	26	22
24p17(e)	Share-based payments	150	107
	Total	**4,099**	2,104

24p18(b) In addition to the above amounts, the Group is committed to pay the members of the Executive Committee up to C1,250 in the event of a change in control of the Group.

24p18(b), 1p77 *(d) Year-end balances arising from sales/purchases of goods/services*

	2013	2012
Receivables from related parties (note 21):		
– Associates	26	32
– Associates of G Limited	24	8
– Ultimate parent	50	40
– Close family members of key management personnel	4	6
Payables to related parties (note 30):		
– Immediate parent	200	190
– Associates	2,902	1,005
– Entity controlled by key management personnel	100	–

The receivables from related parties arise mainly from sale transactions and are due two months after the date of sales. The receivables are unsecured in nature and bear no interest. No provisions are held against receivables from related parties (2012: nil).

The payables to related parties arise mainly from purchase transactions and are due two months after the date of purchase. The payables bear no interest.

(All amounts in C thousands unless otherwise stated)

24p18, 1p77   *(e) Loans to related parties*

	2013	2012
Loans to key management of the company (and their families)[1]:		
At 1 January	196	168
Loans advanced during year	343	62
Loan repayments received	(49)	(34)
Interest charged	30	16
Interest received	(30)	(16)
At 31 December	490	196
Loans to associates:		
At 1 January	1,192	1,206
Loans advanced during year	1,000	50
Loan repayments received	(14)	(64)
Interest charged	187	120
Interest received	(187)	(120)
At 31 December	2,178	1,192
Total loans to related parties:		
At 1 January	1,388	1,374
Loans advanced during year	1,343	112
Loan repayments received	(63)	(98)
Interest charged (note 11)	217	136
Interest received	(217)	(136)
At 31 December (note 21)	2,668	1,388

24p18(b)(i)   The loans advanced to key management have the following terms and conditions:

Name of key management	Amount of loan	Term	Interest rate
2013			
Mr Brown	173	Repayable monthly over 2 years	6.3%
Mr White	170	Repayable monthly over 2 years	6.3%
2012			
Mr Black	20	Repayable monthly over 2 years	6.5%
Mr White	42	Repayable monthly over 1 year	6.5%

IFRS7p15   Certain loans advanced to associates during the year amounting to C1,500 (2012: C500) are collateralised by shares in listed companies. The fair value of these shares was C65 at the end of the reporting period (2012: C590).

The loans to associates are due on 1 January 2014 and carry interest at 7.0% (2012:8%). The fair values and the effective interest rates of loans to associates are disclosed in note 21.

24p18(c)   No provision was required in 2013 (2012: nil) for the loans made to key management personnel and associates

---

[1] None of the loans made to members of key management has been made to directors.

Notes to the consolidated financial statements

(All amounts in C thousands unless otherwise stated)

42 Events after the reporting period

(a) Business combinations

10p21,IFRS3
B64(a)-(d)

The group acquired 100% of the share capital of K&Co, a group of companies specialising in the manufacture of shoes for extreme sports, for a cash consideration of C5,950 on 1 February 2014.

Details of net assets acquired and goodwill are as follows:

	On acquisition
IFRS3B64(f)(i) Purchase consideration:	
– Cash paid	5,950
IFRS3B64(m) – Direct cost relating to acquisition – charged in the income statement	150
7p40(a) Total purchase consideration	5,950
Fair value of assets acquired (see below)	(5,145)
Goodwill	805

IFRS3B64(e)

The above goodwill is attributable to K&Co's strong position and profitability in trading in the niche market for extreme sports equipment.

IFRS3B64(i)

The assets and liabilities arising from the acquisition, provisionally determined, are as follows:

	Fair value
Cash and cash equivalents	195
Property, plant and equipment	31,580
Trademarks	1,000
Licences	700
Customer relationships	1,850
Favourable lease agreements	800
Inventories	995
Trade and other receivables	855
Trade and other payables	(9,646)
Retirement benefit obligations	(1,425)
Borrowings	(19,259)
Deferred tax liabilities	(2,500)
Net assets acquired	5,145

(b) Associates

10p21

The group acquired 40% of the share capital of L&Co, a group of companies specialising in the manufacture of leisure shoes, for a cash consideration of C2,050 on 25 January 2014.

(All amounts in C thousands unless otherwise stated)

Details of net assets acquired and goodwill are as follows:

	On acquisition
Purchase consideration:	
– Cash paid	2,050
– Direct cost relating to acquisition	70
Total purchase consideration	2,120
Share of fair value of net assets acquired (see below)	(2,000)
Goodwill	120

DV

The goodwill is attributable to L&Co's strong position and profitability in trading in the market of leisure shoes and to its workforce, which cannot be separately recognised as an intangible asset.

DV

The assets and liabilities arising from the acquisition, provisionally determined, are as follows:

	Fair value
Contractual customer relationships	380
Property, plant and equipment	3,200
Inventory	500
Cash	220
Trade creditors	(420)
Borrowings	(1,880)
Net assets acquired	2,000

(c) Equity transactions

10p21,
33p71(e),
10p21,
10p22(f)

On 1 January 2014, 1,200 thousand share options were granted to directors and employees with an exercise price set at the market share prices less 15% on that date of C3.13 per share (share price: C3.68) (expiry date: 31 December 2017).

The company re-issued 500,000 treasury shares for a total consideration of C1,500 on 15 January 2014.

(d) Borrowings

10p21

On 1 February 2014, the group issued C6,777 6.5% US dollar bonds to finance its expansion programme and working capital requirements in the US. The bonds are repayable on 31 December 2017.

43 Changes in accounting policies

IFRS GAAP plc adopted IFRS 10, 'Consolidated financial statements', IFRS 11, 'Joint arrangements', IFRS 12, 'Disclosure of interests in other entities', and consequential amendments to IAS 28, 'Investments in associates and joint ventures' and IAS 27, 'Separate financial statements', on 1 January 2012. The group has also adopted IAS 19 (revised 2011), 'Employee benefits' on 1 January 2012. The new accounting policies has had the following impact on the financial statements.

Notes to the consolidated financial statements

(All amounts in C thousands unless otherwise stated)

(a) Consolidation of entities in which the group holds less than 50%

The group is the largest shareholder of Delta Inc with a 40% equity interest, while all other shareholders individually own less than 1% of its equity shares. There is no history of other shareholders forming a group to exercise their votes collectively. Based on the absolute size of the group's shareholding and the relative size of the other shareholdings, management have concluded that the group has sufficiently dominant voting interest to have the power to direct the relevant activities of the entity. As a result the entity has been fully consolidated into these financial statements. Previously Delta Inc was classified as an associate of the group and accounted for using the equity method.

(b) Joint ventures accounted for using the equity method

The group has joint control over Gamma Limited by virtue of its 50% share in the equity shares of the company and the requirement for unanimous consent by all parites over decisions related to the relevant activities of the arrangement. The investment has been classified as a joint venture under IFRS 11 and therefore the equity method of accounting has been used in the consolidated financial statements. Prior to the adoption of IFRS 11, the group's interest in Gamma Limited was proportionately consolidated.

The group recognised its investment in the joint venture at the beginning of the earliest period presented (1 January 2012), as the total of the carrying amounts of the assets and liabilities previously proportionately consolidated by the group. This is the deemed cost of the group's investment in the joint venture for applying equity accounting.

(c) Adoption of IAS 19 (revised 2011)

The revised employee benefit standard introduces changes to the recognition, measurement, presentation and disclosure of post-employment benefits. The standard also requires net interest expense / income to be calculated as the product of the net defined benefit liability / asset and the discount rate as determined at the beginning of the year. The effect of this is to remove the previous concept of recognising an expected return on plan assets.

The effects of the changes to the accounting policies is shown in the following tables.

Page deliberately left blank

(All amounts in C thousands unless otherwise stated)

Impact of change in accounting policy on consolidated balance sheet

		As at 31 December 2013	Consoli- dation of Delta Inc	Equity accounting for Gamma Limited	Adopt IAS 19 (revised 2011)	As at 31 December 2013 as presented
8p28	**Assets**					
	Non-current assets					
	Property, plant and equipment	153,590	6,351	(4,600)	–	155,341
	Intangible assets	25,339	1,841	(908)	–	26,272
	Investments accounted for using the equity method	18,542	(5,169)	5,276	–	18,649
	Deferred income tax asset	3,520	–	–	26	3,546
	Available-for-sale financial assets	17,420	–	–	–	17,420
	Derivative financial instruments	395	–	–	–	395
	Trade and other receivables	2,322	–	–	–	2,322
		221,128	3,023	(232)	26	223,945
	Current assets					
	Inventories	25,058	1,471	(1,829)	–	24,700
	Trade and other receivables	19,490	2,130	(1,855)	–	19,765
	Available-for-sale financial assets	1,950	–	–	–	1,950
	Derivative financial instruments	1,069	–	–	–	1,069
	Financial assets at fair value through profit or loss	11,820	–	–	–	11,820
	Cash and cash equivalents (excluding bank overdrafts)	17,549	969	(590)	–	17,928
		76,936	4,570	(4,274)	–	77,232
	Assets of disposal group	3,333	–	–	–	3,333
		80,269	4,570	(4,274)	–	80,565
	Total assets	301,397	7,593	(4,506)	26	304,510

(All amounts in C thousands unless otherwise stated)

As at 31 December 2012 (previously stated)	Consoli- dation of Delta Inc	Equity accounting for Gamma Limited	Adopt IAS 19 (revised 2011)	As at 31 December 2012 (restated)	As at 1 January 2012 (previously stated)	Consoli- dation of Delta Inc	Equity accounting for Gamma Limited	Adopt IAS 19 (revised 2011)	As at 1 January 2012 (restated)
98,399	5,844	(4,010)	–	100,233	106,750	3,924	(3,460)	–	107,214
19,763	1,820	(883)	–	20,700	20,576	1,744	(858)	–	21,462
17,979	(4,735)	3,809	–	17,053	16,834	(3,826)	2,932	–	15,940
3,321	–	–	62	3,383	2,832	–	–	47	2,879
14,910	–	–	–	14,910	13,222	–	–	–	13,222
245	–	–	–	245	187	–	–	–	187
1,352	–	–	–	1,352	1,106	–	–	–	1,106
155,969	2,929	(1,084)	62	157,876	161,507	1,842	(1,386)	47	162,010
17,845	1,607	(1,270)	–	18,182	16,751	1,447	(925)	–	17,273
17,237	2,211	(1,118)	–	18,330	15,709	1,573	(683)	–	16,599
–	–	–	–	–	–	–	–	–	–
951	–	–	–	951	980	–	–	–	980
7,972	–	–	–	7,972	7,342	–	–	–	7,342
34,130	322	(390)	–	34,062	22,090	234	(192)	–	22,132
78,135	4,140	(2,778)	–	79,497	62,872	3,254	(1,800)	–	64,326
–	–	–	–	–	–	–	–	–	–
78,135	4,140	(2,778)	–	79,497	62,872	3,254	(1,800)	–	64,326
234,104	7,069	(3,862)	62	237,373	224,379	5,096	(3,186)	47	226,336

(All amounts in C thousands unless otherwise stated)

	As at 31 December 2013	Consoli- dation of Delta Inc	Equity accounting for Gamma Limited	Adopt IAS 19 (revised 2011)	As at 31 December 2013 as presented
Equity and liabilities					
Equity attributable to equity holders of the company					
Ordinary shares	25,300	–	–	–	25,300
Share premium	17,144	–	–	–	17,144
Other reserves	11,435	–	–	177	11,612
Retained earnings	75,282	–	–	(632)	74,650
	129,161	–	–	(455)	128,706
Non-controlling interests	6,846	1,042	–	–	7,888
Total equity	136,007	1,042	–	(455)	136,594
Liabilities					
Non-current liabilities					
Borrowings	114,730	3,812	(3,421)	–	115,121
Derivative financial instruments	135	–	–	–	135
Deferred income tax liabilities	12,370	–	–	–	12,370
Retirement benefit obligations	4,635	–	–	481	5,116
Provisions for other liabilities and charges	339	65	(88)	–	316
	132,209	3,877	(3,509)	481	133,058
Current liabilities					
Trade and other payables	16,121	870	(321)	–	16,670
Current income tax liabilities	2,125	540	(99)	–	2,566
Borrowings	11,810	458	(552)	–	11,716
Derivative financial instruments	460	–	–	–	460
Provisions for other liabilities and charges	2,445	806	(25)	–	3,226
	32,961	2,674	(997)	–	34,638
Liabilities of disposal group	220	–	–	–	220
	33,181	2,674	(997)	–	34,858
Total liabilities	165,390	6,551	(4,506)	481	167,916
Total equity and liabilities	301,397	7,593	(4,506)	26	304,510

(All amounts in C thousands unless otherwise stated)

As at 31 December 2012 (previously stated)	Consoli-dation of Delta Inc	Equity accounting for Gamma Limited	Adopt IAS 19 (revised 2011)	As at 31 December 2012 (restated)	As at 1 January 2012 (previously stated)	Consoli-dation of Delta Inc	Equity accounting for Gamma Limited	Adopt IAS 19 (revised 2011)	As at 1 January 2012 (restated)
21,000	–	–	–	21,000	20,000	–	–	–	20,000
10,494	–	–	–	10,494	10,424	–	–	–	10,424
7,005	–	–	189	7,194	6,263	–	–	101	6,364
52,490	–	–	(505)	51,985	51,456	–	–	(331)	51,125
90,989	–	–	(316)	90,673	88,143	–	–	(230)	87,913
984	782	–	–	1,766	1,263	237	–	–	1,500
91,973	782	–	(316)	92,439	89,406	237	–	(230)	89,413
95,682	3,518	(2,854)	–	96,346	66,315	1,801	(2,332)	–	65,784
129	–	–	–	129	130	–	–	–	130
9,053	–	–	–	9,053	5,926	–	–	–	5,926
2,233	–	–	378	2,611	1,559	–	–	277	1,836
353	19	(98)	–	274	184	77	(11)	–	250
107,450	3,537	(2,952)	378	108,413	74,114	1,878	(2,343)	277	73,926
11,964	755	(241)	–	12,478	10,568	650	(187)	–	11,031
2,232	632	(93)	–	2,771	6,765	543	(89)	–	7,219
17,889	916	(547)	–	18,258	41,903	995	(542)	–	42,356
618	–	–	–	618	520	–	–	–	520
1,978	447	(29)	–	2,396	1,103	793	(25)	–	1,871
34,681	2,750	(910)	–	36,521	60,859	2,981	(843)	–	62,997
–	–	–	–	–	–	–	–	–	–
34,681	2,750	(910)	–	36,521	60,859	2,981	(843)	–	62,997
142,131	6,287	(3,862)	378	144,934	134,973	4,859	(3,186)	277	136,923
234,104	7,069	(3,862)	62	237,373	224,379	5,096	(3,186)	47	226,336

Notes to the consolidated financial statements

(All amounts in C thousands unless otherwise stated)

Impact of change in accounting policy on the consolidated income statement

8p28

	For period ended 31 December 2013	Consolidation of Delta Inc	Equity accounting for Gamma Limited	Adopt IAS 19 (revised 2011)	For period ended 31 December 2013 as presented
Continuing operations					
Revenue	206,085	16,759	(11,810)	–	211,034
Cost of sales	(70,977)	(11,797)	5,408	–	(77,366)
Gross profit	135,108	4,962	(6,402)	–	133,668
Distribution costs	(52,054)	(1,354)	879	–	(52,529)
Administrative expenses	(29,231)	(2,535)	1,871	(210)	(30,105)
Other income	2,750	–	–	–	2,750
Other (losses)/gains- net	(90)	–	–	–	(90)
Operating profit	56,483	1,073	(3,652)	(210)	53,694
Finance income	1,796	37	(103)	–	1,730
Finance costs	(8,578)	(475)	880	–	(8,173)
Finance costs–net	(6,782)	(438)	777	–	(6,443)
Share of profit of investments accounted for using the equity method	389	(174)	1467	–	1,682
Profit before income tax	50,090	461	(1,408)	(210)	48,933
Income tax expense	(15,881)	(201)	1408	63	(14,611)
Profit for the year from continuing operations	34,209	260	–	(147)	34,322
Discontinued operations					
Profit for the year from discontinued operations (attributable to equity holders of the company)	100	–	–	–	100
Profit for the year	34,309	260	–	(147)	34,422

(All amounts in C thousands unless otherwise stated)

For period ended 31 December 2012	Consolidation of Delta Inc	Equity accounting for Gamma Limited	Adopt IAS 19 (revised 2011)	For period ended 31 December 2012 (Restated)
106,693	17,246	(11,579)	–	112,360
(40,373)	(11,896)	5,587	–	(46,682)
66,320	5,350	(5,992)	–	65,678
(20,795)	(1,421)	1,003	–	(21,213)
(9,896)	(2,089)	1,559	(85)	(10,511)
1,259	–	–	–	1,259
63	–	–	–	63
36,951	1,840	(3,430)	(85)	35,276
1,891	42	(324)	–	1,609
(12,933)	(415)	1151	–	(12,197)
(11,042)	(373)	827	–	(10,588)
509	(364)	877	–	1,022
26,418	1,103	(1,726)	(85)	25,710
(9,864)	(558)	1726	26	(8,670)
16,554	545	–	(59)	17,040
120	–	–	–	120
16,674	545	–	(59)	17,160

Notes to the consolidated financial statements

(All amounts in C thousands unless otherwise stated)

Impact of change in accounting policy on the consolidated statement of comprehensive income

	For period ended 31 December 2013	Consolidation of Delta Inc	Equity accounting for Gamma Limited	Adopt IAS 19 (revised 2011)	For period ended 31 December 2013 as presented
Profit for the year	34,309	260	–	(147)	34,422
Other comprehensive income:					
Items that will not be reclassified to profit or loss					
Gains on revaluation of land and buildings	755	–	–	–	755
Remeasurements ofpost employment benefit obligations	0	–	–	83	83
	755	–	–	83	838
Items that may be subsequently reclassified to profit or loss					
Change in value of available-for-sale financial assets	362	–	–	–	362
Reclassification of revaluation of previously held interest in ABC Group	(850)	–	–	–	(850)
Share of other comprehensive income of associates	(86)	–	–	–	(86)
Impact of change in Euravian tax rate on deferred tax	(10)	–	–	–	(10)
Cash flow hedges	64	–	–	–	64
Net investment hedge	(45)	–	–	–	(45)
Currency translation differences	2,413	–	–	(12)	2,401
	1,848	–	–	(12)	1,836
Other comprehensive income for the year, net of tax	2,603	–	–	71	2,674
Total comprehensive income for the year	36,912	260	–	(76)	37,096
Attributable to:					
– Owners of the parent	34,372	–	–	(76)	34,296
– Non-controlling interests	2,540	260	–	–	2,800
Total comprehensive income for the year	36,912	260	–	(76)	37,096
Total comprehensive income attributable to equity shareholders arises from:					
– Continuing operations	34,272	–	–	(76)	34,196
– Discontinued operations	100	–	–	–	100
	34,372	–	–	(76)	34,296

(All amounts in C thousands unless otherwise stated)

For period ended 31 December 2012	Consolidation of Delta Inc	Equity accounting for Gamma Limited	Adopt IAS 19 (revised 2011)	For period ended 31 December 2012 (Restated)
16,674	545	–	(59)	17,160
759	–	–	–	759
(494)	–	–	(143)	(637)
265	–	–	(143)	122
912	–	–	–	912
–	–	–	–	–
91	–	–	–	91
–	–	–	–	–
(3)	–	–	–	(3)
40	–	–	–	40
(1,111)	–	–	189	(922)
(71)	–	–	189	118
194	–	–	46	240
16,868	545	–	(13)	17,400
16,597	–	–	(13)	16,584
271	545	–	–	816
16,868	545	–	(13)	17,400
16,477	–	–	(13)	16,464
120	–	–	–	120
16,597	–	–	(13)	16,584

Notes to the consolidated financial statements

(All amounts in C thousands unless otherwise stated)

Impact of change in accounting policy on the consolidated statement of cash flows

	For period ended 31 December 2013	Consolidation of Delta Inc	Equity accounting for Gamma Limited	Adopt IAS 19 (revised 2011)	For period ended 31 December 2013 as presented
Cash flows from operating activities					
Cash generated from operations	76,652	1,522	(3,423)	–	74,751
Interest paid	(8,187)	(483)	835	–	(7,835)
Income tax paid	(16,044)	(186)	1,321	–	(14,909)
Net cash generated from operating activities	52,421	853	(1,267)	–	52,007
Cash flows from investing activities					
Acquisition of subsidiary, net of cash acquired	(3,750)	–	–	–	(3,750)
Purchases of property, plant and equipment	(9,021)	(1,363)	879	–	(9,505)
Proceeds from sale of property, plant and equipment	6,296	90	(32)	–	6,354
Purchases of intangible assets	(2,990)	(165)	105	–	(3,050)
Purchases of available-for-sale financial assets	(4,887)	–	–	–	(4,887)
Proceeds from disposal of available-for-sale financial assets	151	–	–	–	151
Loans granted to related parties	(1,343)	–	–	–	(1,343)
Loan repayments received from related parties	63	–	–	–	63
Interest received	1,077	72	(95)	–	1,054
Dividends received	1,130	–	–	–	1,130
Net cash used in investing activities	(13,274)	(1,366)	857	–	(13,783)

(All amounts in C thousands unless otherwise stated)

For period ended 31 December 2012	Consolidation of Delta Inc	Equity accounting for Gamma Limited	Adopt IAS 19 (revised 2011)	For period ended 31 December 2012 (Restated)
42,453	1,925	(2,675)	–	41,703
(15,437)	(381)	1,045	–	(14,773)
(11,639)	(358)	1,471	–	(10,526)
15,377	1,186	(159)	–	16,404
–	–	–	–	–
(4,915)	(2,033)	906	–	(6,042)
2,910	193	(124)	–	2,979
(928)	107	121	–	(700)
(1,150)	–	–	–	(1,150)
–	–	–	–	–
(112)	–	–	–	(112)
98	–	–	–	98
1,371	29	(207)	–	1,193
1,120	–	–	–	1,120
(1,606)	(1,704)	696	–	(2,614)

Notes to the consolidated financial statements

(All amounts in C thousands unless otherwise stated)

	For period ended 31 December 2013	Consolidation of Delta Inc	Equity accounting for Gamma Limited	Adopt IAS 19 (revised 2011)	For period ended 31 December 2013 as presented
Cash flows from financing activities					
Proceeds from issuance of ordinary shares	950	–	–	–	950
Purchase of treasury shares	(2,564)	–	–	–	(2,564)
Proceeds from issuance of convertible bonds	50,000	–	–	–	50,000
Proceeds from issuance of redeemable preference shares	–	–	–	–	–
Proceeds from borrowings	9,500	–	(1,000)	–	8,500
Repayments of borrowings	(94,429)	(253)	689	–	(93,993)
Dividends paid to owners of the parent	(10,102)	–	–	–	(10,102)
Dividends paid to holders of redeemable preference shares	(1,950)	–	–	–	(1,950)
Acquisition of interest in a subsidiary	(1,100)	–	–	–	(1,100)
Sale of interest in a subsidiary	1,100	–	–	–	1,100
Dividends paid to non-controlling interests	(1,920)	–	–	–	(1,920)
Net cash used in financing activities	**(50,515)**	**(253)**	**(311)**	**–**	**(51,079)**
Net (decrease)/increase in cash and cash equivalents	**(11,368)**	**(766)**	**(721)**	**–**	**(12,855)**
Cash and cash equivalents at beginning of year	27,666	322	(390)	–	27,598
Exchange gains/(losses) on cash and cash equivalents	(1,399)	1,413	521	–	535
Cash and cash equivalent at end of year	**14,899**	**969**	**(590)**	**–**	**15,278**

(All amounts in C thousands unless otherwise stated)

For period ended 31 December 2012	Consolidation of Delta Inc	Equity accounting for Gamma Limited	Adopt IAS 19 (revised 2011)	For period ended 31 December 2012 (Restated)
1,070	–	–	–	1,070
–	–	–	–	–
–	–	–	–	–
30,000	–	–	–	30,000
16,536	2,214	(750)	–	18,000
(34,737)	(245)	308	–	(34,674)
(15,736)	–	–	–	(15,736)
(1,950)	–	–	–	(1,950)
–	–	–	–	–
–	–	–	–	–
(550)	–	–	–	(550)
(5,367)	1,969	(442)	–	(3,840)
8,404	1,451	95	–	9,950
17,545	234	(192)	–	17,587
1,717	(1,363)	(293)	–	61
27,666	322	(390)	–	27,598

(All amounts in C thousands unless otherwise stated)

Impact of change in accounting policy on the statement of changes in equity

	Attributable to owners of the parent					Non-controlling interest	Total equity
	Share capital	Share premium	Other reserves	Retained earnings	Total		
Balance as at 1 January 2012 as previously reported	20,000	10,424	6,263	51,456	88,143	1,263	89,406
Effect of changes in accounting policies	–	–	101	(331)	(230)	237	7
Balance as at 1 January 2012 as restated	20,000	10,424	6,364	51,125	87,913	1,500	89,413
Profit for the year as previously reported	–	–	–	16,363	16,363	311	16,674
Effect of changes in accounting policies	–	–	–	(59)	(59)	545	486
Profit for the year as restated	–	–	–	16,304	16,304	856	17,160
Other comprehensive income for the year as previously reported	–	–	784	(550)	234	(40)	194
Effect of changes in accounting policies	–	–	46	–	46	–	46
Other comprehensive income for the year as restated	–	–	830	(550)	280	(40)	240
Total comprehensive income for the year as previously reported	–	–	784	15,813	16,597	271	16,868
Effect of changes in accounting policies	–	–	46	(59)	(13)	545	532
Total comprehensive income for the year	–	–	830	15,754	16,584	816	17,400
Value of employee services[1]	–	–	–	822	822	–	822
Tax credit relating to share option scheme[1]	–	–	–	20	20	–	20
Proceeds from shares issued[1]	1,000	70	–	–	1,070	–	1,070
Dividends[1]	–	–	–	(15,736)	(15,736)	(550)	(16,286)
Total contributions by and distributions to owners of the parent, recognised directly in equity[1]	1,000	70	–	(14,894)	(13,824)	(550)	(14,374)
Balance as at 31 December 2012 as previously reported	21,000	10,494	7,047	52,375	90,916	984	91,900
Effect of changes in accounting policies	–	–	147	(390)	(243)	782	539
Balance as at 31 December 2012	21,000	10,494	7,194	51,985	90,673	1,766	92,439

[1] There is no impact on these financial statement line items for the change in the accounting policies.

(All amounts in C thousands unless otherwise stated)

Independent auditor's report to the shareholders of IFRS GAAP plc

Report on the consolidated financial statements

We have audited the accompanying consolidated financial statements of IFRS GAAP plc, which comprise the consolidated balance sheet as at 31 December 2013 and the consolidated statements of income, comprehensive income, changes in equity and cash flows for the year then ended, and a summary of significant accounting policies and other explanatory notes.

Management's responsibility for the consolidated financial statements

Management is responsible for the preparation of consolidated financial statements that give a true and fair view in accordance with International Financial Reporting Standards (IFRSs)[1], and for such internal control as management determines is necessary to enable the preparation of consolidated financial statements that are free from material misstatement, whether due to fraud or error.

Auditor's responsibility

Our responsibility is to express an opinion on these consolidated financial statements based on our audit. We conducted our audit in accordance with International Standards on Auditing. Those standards require that we comply with ethical requirements and plan and perform the audit to obtain reasonable assurance about whether the consolidated financial statements are free from material misstatement.

An audit involves performing procedures to obtain audit evidence about the amounts and disclosures in the consolidated financial statements. The procedures selected depend on the auditor's judgement, including the assessment of the risks of material misstatement of the consolidated financial statements, whether due to fraud or error. In making those risk assessments, the auditor considers internal control relevant to the entity's preparation of consolidated financial statements that give a true and fair view[2] in order to design audit procedures that are appropriate in the circumstances, but not for the purpose of expressing an opinion on the effectiveness of the entity's internal control. An audit also includes evaluating the appropriateness of accounting policies used and the reasonableness of accounting estimates made by management, as well as evaluating the overall presentation of the consolidated financial statements.

We believe that the audit evidence we have obtained is sufficient and appropriate to provide a basis for our audit opinion.

Opinion

In our opinion, the accompanying consolidated financial statements give a true and fair view[3] of the financial position of IFRS GAAP plc and its subsidiaries as at 31 December 2013, and of their financial performance and cash flows for the year then ended in accordance with International Financial Reporting Standards (IFRSs).

---

[1] This can be changed to say, 'Management is responsible for the preparation and fair presentation of these financial statements in accordance...' where the term 'true and fair view' is not used.

[2] This can be changed to say '...relevant to the entity's preparation and fair presentation of the consolidated financial statements in order...' where the term 'true and fair view' is not used.

[3] The term 'give a true and fair view of' can be changed to 'present fairly, in all material aspects'.

Independent auditor's report to the shareholders of IFRS GAAP plc

(All amounts in C thousands unless otherwise stated)

Report on other legal and regulatory requirements

[Form and content of this section of the auditor's report will vary depending on the nature of the auditor's other reporting responsibilities, if any.]

Auditor's signature
Date of the auditor's report
Auditor's address

[The format of the audit report will need to be tailored to reflect the legal framework of particular countries. In certain countries, the audit report covers both the current year and the comparative year.]

(All amounts in C thousands unless otherwise stated)

Appendix I – Operating and financial review; management commentary

International Organization of Securities Commissions

In 1998, the International Organization of Securities Commissions (IOSCO) issued 'International disclosure standards for cross- border offerings and initial listings by foreign issuers', comprising recommended disclosure standards, including an operating and financial review and discussion of future prospects. IOSCO standards for prospectuses are not mandatory, but they are increasingly incorporated in national stock exchange requirements for prospectuses and annual reports. The text of IOSCO's standard on operating and financial reviews and prospects is reproduced below. Although the standard refers to a 'company' throughout, we consider that, where a company has subsidiaries, it should be applied to the group.

Standard

Discuss the company's financial condition, changes in financial condition and results of operations for each year and interim period for which financial statements are required, including the causes of material changes from year to year in financial statement line items, to the extent necessary for an understanding of the company's business as a whole. Information provided also shall relate to all separate segments of the group. Provide the information specified below as well as such other information that is necessary for an investor's understanding of the company's financial condition, changes in financial condition and results of operations.

A Operating results. Provide information regarding significant factors, including unusual or infrequent events or new developments, materially affecting the company's income from operations, indicating the extent to which income was so affected. Describe any other significant component of revenue or expenses necessary to understand the company's results of operations.

(1) To the extent that the financial statements disclose material changes in net sales or revenues, provide a narrative discussion of the extent to which such changes are attributable to changes in prices or to changes in the volume or amount of products or services being sold or to the introduction of new products or services.

(2) Describe the impact of inflation, if material. If the currency in which financial statements are presented is of a country that has experienced hyperinflation, the existence of such inflation, a five-year history of the annual rate of inflation and a discussion of the impact of hyperinflation on the company's business shall be disclosed.

(3) Provide information regarding the impact of foreign currency fluctuations on the company, if material, and the extent to which foreign currency net investments are hedged by currency borrowings and other hedging instruments.

(4) Provide information regarding any governmental economic, fiscal, monetary or political policies or factors that have materially affected, or could materially affect, directly or indirectly, the company's operations or investments by host country shareholders.

B Liquidity and capital resources. The following information shall be provided:

(1) Information regarding the company's liquidity (both short and long term), including:

(a) a description of the internal and external sources of liquidity and a brief discussion of any material unused sources of liquidity. Include a statement by the company that, in its opinion, the working capital is sufficient for the company's present requirements, or, if not, how it proposes to provide the additional working capital needed.

(All amounts in C thousands unless otherwise stated)

(b) an evaluation of the sources and amounts of the company's cash flows, including the nature and extent of any legal or economic restrictions on the ability of subsidiaries to transfer funds to the parent in the form of cash dividends, loans or advances and the impact such restrictions have had or are expected to have on the ability of the company to meet its cash obligations.

(c) information on the level of borrowings at the end of the period under review, the seasonality of borrowing requirements and the maturity profile of borrowings and committed borrowing facilities, with a description of any restrictions on their use.

(2) Information regarding the type of financial instruments used, the maturity profile of debt, currency and interest rate structure. The discussion also should include funding and treasury policies and objectives in terms of the manner in which treasury activities are controlled, the currencies in which cash and cash equivalents are held, the extent to which borrowings are at fixed rates, and the use of financial instruments for hedging purposes.

(3) Information regarding the company's material commitments for capital expenditures as of the end of the latest financial year and any subsequent interim period and an indication of the general purpose of such commitments and the anticipated sources of funds needed to fulfil such commitments.

C Research and development, patents and licenses, etc. Provide a description of the company's research and development policies for the last three years, where it is significant, including the amount spent during each of the last three financial years on group-sponsored research and development activities.

D Trend information. The group should identify the most significant recent trends in production, sales and inventory, the state of the order book and costs and selling prices since the latest financial year. The group also should discuss, for at least the current financial year, any known trends, uncertainties, demands, commitments or events that are reasonably likely to have a material effect on the group's net sales or revenues, income from continuing operations, profitability, liquidity or capital resources, or that would cause reported financial information not necessarily to be indicative of future operating results or financial condition.

Management commentary

The IASB issued a non-mandatory practice statement on management commentary in December 2010 that provides principles for the presentation of a narrative report on an entity's financial performance, position and cash flows.

The IASB's practice statement provides a broad framework of principles, qualitative characteristics and elements that might be used to provide users of financial reports with decision-useful information. The practice statement recommends that the commentary is entity-specific and may include the following components:

- A description of the business including discussion of matters such as the industries, markets and competitive position; legal, regulatory and macro-economic environment; and the entity's structure and economic model.
- Management's objectives and strategies to help users understand the priorities for action and the resources that must be managed to deliver results.
- The critical financial and non-financial resources available to the entity and how those resources are used in meeting management's objectives for the entity.
- The principal risks, and management's plans and strategies for managing those risks, and the effectiveness of those strategies.

(All amounts in C thousands unless otherwise stated)

- The performance and development of the entity to provide insights into the trends and factors affecting the business and to help users understand the extent to which past performance may be indicative of future performance.
- The performance measures that management uses to evaluate the entity's performance against its objectives, which helps users to assess the degree to which goals and objectives are being achieved.

(All amounts in C thousands unless otherwise stated)

Appendix II – Alternative presentation of primary statements

> This appendix is independent of the illustrative financial statements in the main body of IFRS GAAP Plc. The figures do not have any correlation with those in the main body and hence should not be compared.

Consolidated statement of cash flows – direct method

IAS 7 encourages the use of the 'direct method' for the presentation of cash flows from operating activities. The presentation of cash flows from operating activities using the direct method in accordance with IAS 7p18 is as follows:

Consolidated statement of cash flows

1p113, 7p10

		Year ended 31 December	
		2013	2012 Restated
7p18(a)	**Cash flows from operating activities**		
	Cash receipts from customers	**212,847**	114,451
	Cash paid to suppliers and employees	**(156,613)**	(72,675)
	Cash generated from operations	**56,234**	41,776
	Interest paid	**(7,835)**	(14,773)
	Income taxes paid	**(16,909)**	(10,526)
	Net cash flows from operating activities	**31,490**	16,477
7p21,7p10	**Cash flows from investing activities**		
7p39	Acquisition of subsidiary, net of cash acquired	**(3,950)**	–
7p16(a)	Purchases of property, plant and equipment	**(9,755)**	(6,042)
7p16(b)	Proceeds from sale of property, plant and equipment	**6,354**	2,979
7p16(a)	Purchases of intangible assets	**(3,050)**	(700)
7p16(c)	Purchases of available-for-sale financial assets	**(2,781)**	(1,126)
7p16(e)	Loans granted to associates	**(1,000)**	(50)
7p16(f)	Loan repayments received from associates	**14**	64
7p31	Interest received	**1,054**	1,193
7p31	Dividends received	**1,130**	1,120
	Net cash used in investing activities	**(11,984)**	(2,562)
7p21,7p10	**Cash flows from financing activities**		
7p17(a)	Proceeds from issuance of ordinary shares	**950**	1,070
7p17(b)	Purchase of treasury shares	**(2,564)**	–
7p17(c)	Proceeds from issuance of convertible bond	**50,000**	–
7p17(c)	Proceeds from issuance of redeemable preference shares	**–**	30,000
7p17(c)	Proceeds from borrowings	**8,500**	18,000
7p17(d)	Repayments of borrowings	**(78,117)**	(34,674)
7p31	Dividends paid to owners of the parent	**(10,102)**	(15,736)
7p31	Dividends paid to holders of redeemable preference shares	**(1,950)**	(1,950)
7p31	Dividends paid to non-controlling interests	**(1,920)**	(550)
	Net cash used in financing activities	**(35,203)**	(3,840)
	Net (decrease)/increase in cash, cash equivalents and bank overdrafts	**(15,697)**	10,075
7p28	Cash, cash equivalents and bank overdrafts at beginning of the year	**27,598**	17,587
	Exchange gains/(losses) on cash, cash equivalents and bank overdrafts	**535**	(64)
7p28	**Cash, cash equivalents and bank overdrafts at end of the year**	**12,436**	27,598

The notes on pages XX to XXX are an integral part of these consolidated financial statements.

(All amounts in C thousands unless otherwise stated)

Consolidated statement of comprehensive income – single statement, showing expenses by function

		Year ended 31 December	
1p10(b),10A		**2013**	2012 Restated
	Continuing operations		
1p82(a)	Revenue	**211,034**	112,360
1p99, 1p103	Cost of sales	**(77,366)**	(46,682)
1p103	**Gross profit**	**133,668**	65,678
1p99, 1p103	Distribution costs	**(52,529)**	(21,213)
1p99, 1p103	Administrative expenses	**(30,105)**	(10,511)
1p99, 1p103	Other income	**2,750**	1,259
1p85	Other (losses)/gains – net	**(90)**	63
1p85	**Operating profit**	**53,694**	35,276
1p85	Finance income	**1,730**	1,609
1p82(b)	Finance cost	**(8,173)**	(12,197)
1p85	Finance costs – net	**(6,443)**	(10,588)
1p82(c)	Share of profit of invesments accounted for using the equity method	**1,682**	1,022
1p85	**Profit before income tax**	**48,933**	25,710
1p82(d),12p77	Income tax expense	**(14,611)**	(8,670)
1p85	Profit for the year from continuing operations	**34,322**	17,040
IFRS5p33(a)	**Discontinued operations:**		
	Profit for the year from discontinued operations	**100**	120
1p81A(a)	**Profit for the year**	**34,422**	17,160
	Other comprehensive income:		
1p82A	**Items that will not be reclassified to profit or loss**		
16p39	Gains on revaluation of land and buildings	**755**	759
19p93B	Remeasurements of post employment benefit obligations	**83**	(637)
		838	122
1p82A	**Items that may be subsequently reclassified to profit or loss**		
IFRS7p20(a)(ii)	Change in value of available-for-sale financial assets	**362**	912
IFRS3p59	Reclassification of revaluation of previously held interest in ABC Group	**(850)**	–
1p85	Impact of change in the Euravian tax rate on deferred tax	**(10)**	–
IFRS7p23(c)	Cash flow hedges	**64**	(3)
1p85	Net investment hedge	**(45)**	40
21p52(b)	Currency translation differences	**2,401**	(922)
1p82A	Share of other comprehensive income of associates	**(86)**	91
		1,836	118
	Other comprehensive income for the year, net of tax	**2,674**	240
1p81A(c)	**Total comprehensive income for the year**	**37,096**	17,400
	Profit attributable to:		
1p81B(a)(ii)	Owners of the parent	**31,874**	16,304
1p81B(a)(i), IFRS12p12(e)	Non-controlling interests	**2,548**	856
		34,422	17,160

(All amounts in C thousands unless otherwise stated)

		Year ended 31 December	
		2013	2012 Restated
	Total comprehensive income attributable to:		
1p81B(b)(ii)	Equity holders of the company	**34,296**	16,584
1p81B(b)(i)	Non-controlling interest	**2,800**	816
		37,096	17,400
	Total comprehensive income attributable to equity shareholders arises from:		
	Continuing operations	**34,196**	16,464
IFRS5p33(d)	Discontinued operations	**100**	120
		34,296	16,584

Earnings per share from continuing and discontinued operations to the equity holders of the parent during the year (expressed in C per share)

		2013	2012
	Basic earnings per share		
33p66	From continuing operations	**1.35**	0.79
33p68	From discontinued operations	**0.01**	0.01
		1.36	0.8
	Diluted earnings per share[1]		
33p66	From continuing operations	**1.21**	0.74
33p68	From discontinued operations	**0.01**	0.01
		1.22	0.75

The notes on pages XX to XXX are an integral part of these consolidated financial statements.

[1] EPS for discontinued operations may be given in the notes to the accounts instead of the face of the income statement. The income tax effect has been presented on an aggregate basis; therefore an additional note disclosure resents the income tax effect of each component. Alternatively, this information could be presented within the statement of comprehensive income.

(All amounts in C thousands unless otherwise stated)

Appendix III – Areas not illustrated in financial statements of IFRS GAAP plc

1. Biological assets

Note 1 – General information

1p138(b),
41p46(a)
The group is engaged in the business of farming sheep primarily for sale to meat processors. The group is also engaged in the business of growing and managing palm oil plantations for the sale of palm oil. The group earns ancillary income from various agricultural produce, such as wool.

Note 2 – Accounting policies

Basis of preparation

1p117(a)
The consolidated financial statements have been prepared under the historical cost convention, as modified by the revaluation of land and buildings, available-for-sale financial assets, financial assets and financial liabilities (including derivative financial instruments at fair value through profit or loss) and certain biological assets.

1p119
Biological assets

41p41
Biological assets comprise sheep and palm oil plantations.

IFRS13p93(d)
Sheep are measured at fair value less cost to sell, based on market prices at auction of livestock of similar age, breed and genetic merit with adjustments, where necessary, to reflect the differences.

IFRS13p93(d)
The fair value of oil palms excludes the land upon which the trees are planted or the fixed assets utilised in the upkeep of planted areas. The biological process starts with preparation of land for planting seedlings and ends with the harvesting of crops in the form of fresh fruit bunches ('FFB'). Thereafter, crude palm oil and palm kernel oil is extracted from FFB. Consistently with this process, the fair value of oil palms is determined using a discounted cash flow model, by reference to the estimated FFB crop harvest over the full remaining productive life of the trees of up to 20 years, applying an estimated produce value for transfer to the manufacturing process and allowing for upkeep, harvesting costs and an appropriate allocation of overheads. The estimated produce value is derived from a long term forecast of crude palm oil prices to determine the present value of expected future cash flows over the next 20 years. The estimated FFB crop harvest used to derive the fair value is derived by applying palm oil yield to plantation size.

41p54(a),(b)
Costs to sell include the incremental selling costs, including auctioneers' fees and commission paid to brokers and dealers.

Changes in fair value of livestock and palm oil plantations are recognised in the income statement.

Farming costs such as feeding, labour costs, pasture maintenance, veterinary services and sheering are expensed as incurred. The cost of purchase of sheep plus transportation charges are capitalised as part of biological assets.

(All amounts in C thousands unless otherwise stated)

Note 3 – Estimates and judgements – Biological assets

IFRS13p93(d) In measuring the fair value of sheep and palm oil plantations various management estimates and judgements are required:

(a) Sheep

Estimates and judgements in determining the fair value of sheep relate to the market prices, average weight and quality of animals and mortality rates.

Market price of sheep is obtained from the weekly auctions at the local market. The quality of livestock sold at the local market is considered to approximate the group's breeding and slaughter livestock.

The sheep grow at different rates and there can be a considerable spread in the quality and weight of animals and that affects the price achieved. An average weight is assumed for the slaughter sheep livestock that are not yet at marketable weight.

(b) Palm oil plantations

Estimates and judgements in determining the fair value of palm oil plantations relate to determining the palm oil yield, the long term crude palm oil price, palm kernel oil price and the discount rates.

Consolidated income statement (extracts)

		Note	2013	2012
	Revenue	4	**26,240**	27,548
41p40	Change in fair value of biological assets	5	**23,480**	19,028
	Cost of sales of livestock and palm oil	5	**(23,180)**	(24,348)

Consolidated balance sheet (extracts)

		Note	2013	2012
1p68				
	Assets			
1p60	**Non-current assets**			
1p54(f)	Biological assets	5	**37,500**	25,940
1p60	**Current assets**			
1p54(f)	Biological assets	5	**4,300**	5,760

Note 4 – Revenue (extract)

	Note	2013	2012
Sale of livestock and palm oil	5	**23,740**	25,198
Sale of wool		**2,500**	2,350
Total revenue		**26,240**	27,548

(All amounts in C thousands unless otherwise stated)

Note 5 – Biological assets

		2013	2012
41p50	At 1 January	31,700	32,420
41p50(b)	Increase due to purchases	10,280	4,600
41p50(a)	Livestock losses	(480)	(350)
41p50(a)	Change in fair value due to biological transformation	21,950	17,930
41p50(a)	Change in fair value of livestock due to price changes	1,530	1,448
41p50(d)	Transfer of harvested FFB to inventory	(18,450)	(19,450)
41p50(c)	Decrease due to sales	(4,730)	(4,898)
	At 31 December	**41,800**	31,700
41p43, p45	Sheep – at fair value less cost to sell:		
	– Mature	4,300	5,760
	– Immature	8,200	5,690
		12,500	11,450
	Palm oil plantation		
	– Mature – at fair value less cost to sell	29,300	20,250
		29,300	20,250
	At 31 December	**41,800**	31,700

41p46(b) As at 31 December the group had 6,500 sheep and 2,600,000 hectares palm oil plantations (2012: 5,397 sheep and 2,170,000 hectares of palm oil plantations). During the year the group sold 3,123 sheep (2012: 4,098 sheep) and 550,000 kgs of palm oil (2012: 545,000 kgs of palm oil).

41p43 Sheep for slaughter are classified as immature until they are ready for slaughter.

Selling expenses of C560 (2012:C850) were incurred during the year.

Livestock are classified as current assets if they are to be sold within one year. Harvested FFB are transferred to inventory at fair value when harvested.

IFRS13p93 (a-b) The following table presents the group's biological assets that are measured at fair value at 31 December 2013.

	Level 1	Level 2	Level 3	Total
Sheep				
– Mature	–	4,300	–	4,300
– Immature	–	8,200	–	8,200
Palm oil plantation				
– Mature	–	–	29,300	29,300

IFRS13p93(c) There were no transfers between any levels during the year.

(All amounts in C thousands unless otherwise stated)

The movement in the fair value of the assets within level 3 of the hierarchy is as follows:

	Palm oil plantation
Opening balance	20,250
Increases due to expenditure to planted areas	4,309
Decreases due to harvest	(14,115)
Gain in profit or loss arising from biological transformation	18,856
Closing balance	**29,300**

IFRS 13p93(e)(i)	Total gains or losses for the period included in profit or loss for assets held at the end of the reporting period, under 'Change in fair value of biological assets'	18,856
IFRS 13p93(f)	**Change in unrealised gains or losses for the period included in profit or loss for assets held at the end of the reporting period**	16,532

IFRS13p 93(d),(h)(i)

The following unobservable inputs were used to measure the group's palm oil plantation:

Description	Fair value at 31 December 2013	Valuation technique(s)	Unobservable inputs	Range of unobservable inputs (probability – weighted average)	Relationship of unobservable inputs to fair value
Palm oil plantation	6,815	Discounted cash flows	Palm oil yield – tonnes per hectare	20-30 (24) per year	The higher the palm oil yield, the higher the fair value
			Crude palm oil price	US$ 800-1100 (900) per tonne	The higher the market price, the higher the fair value.
			Palm Kernel Oil price	US$ 1000-1200 (1050) per tonne	
			Discount rate	9%-11% (10.5%)	The higher the discount rate, the lower the fair value.

41p49(c)

Note 6 – Financial risk management strategies

The group is exposed to risks arising from environmental and climatic changes, commodity prices and financing risks.

The group's geographic spread of farms allows a high degree of mitigation against adverse climatic conditions such as droughts and floods and disease outbreaks. The group has strong environmental policies and procedures in place to comply with environmental and other laws.

The group is exposed to risks arising from fluctuations in the price and sales volume of sheep. Where possible, the group enters into supply contracts for sheep to ensure sales volumes can be met by meat processing companies. The group has long-term contracts in place for supply of palm oil to its major customers.

(All amounts in C thousands unless otherwise stated)

The seasonal nature of the sheep farming business requires a high level of cash flow in the second half of the year. The group actively manages the working capital requirements and has secured sufficient credit facilities sufficient to meet the cash flow requirements.

41p49(b)   **Note 7 – Commitments**

The group has entered into a contract to acquire 250 breeding sheep at 31 December 2013 for C1,250 (2012: nil).

2. Construction contracts

Note – Accounting policies

11p3   A construction contract is defined by IAS 11, 'Construction contracts', as a contract specifically negotiated for the construction of an asset.

11p22   When the outcome of a construction contract can be estimated reliably and it is probable that the contract will be profitable, contract revenue is recognised over the period of the contract by reference to the stage of completion. Contract costs are recognised as expenses by reference to the stage of completion of the contract activity at the end of the reporting period. When it is probable that total contract costs will exceed total contract revenue, the expected loss is recognised as an expense immediately.

When the outcome of a construction contract cannot be estimated reliably, contract revenue is recognised only to the extent of contract costs incurred that are likely to be recoverable.

Variations in contract work, claims and incentive payments are included in contract revenue to the extent that may have been agreed with the customer and are capable of being reliably measured.

The group uses the 'percentage-of-completion method 'to determine the appropriate amount to recognise in a given period. The stage of completion is measured by reference to the contract costs incurred up to the end of the reporting period as a percentage of total estimated costs for each contract. Costs incurred in the year in connection with future activity on a contract are excluded from contract costs in determining the stage of completion.

On the balance sheet, the group reports the net contract position for each contract as either an asset or a liability. A contract represents an asset where costs incurred plus recognised profits (less recognised losses) exceed progress billings; a contract represents a liability where the opposite is the case.

(All amounts in C thousands unless otherwise stated)

Consolidated balance sheet (extracts)

		Note	2013	2012
1p60	**Current assets**			
1p54(h)	Trade and other receivables	12	**23,303**	20,374
1p60	**Current liabilities**			
1p54(k)	Trade and other payables	21	**17,667**	13,733

Consolidated income statement (extracts)

		Note	2013	2012
11p39(a)	Contract revenue		**58,115**	39,212
11p16	Contract costs		**(54,729)**	(37,084)
1p103	Gross profit		**3,386**	2,128
1p103	Selling and marketing costs		**(386)**	(128)
1p103	Administrative expenses		**(500)**	(400)

Note – Trade and other receivables (extract)[1]

		2013	2012
IFRS7p36, 1p78(b)	Trade receivables	**18,174**	16,944
	Less: Provision for impairment of receivables	**(109)**	(70)
	Trade receivables – net	**18,065**	16,874
11p42(a)	Amounts due from customers for contract work	**1,216**	920
	Prepayments	**1,300**	1,146
1p77, 24p18	Receivables from related parties (note 41)	**54**	46
1p77, 24p18	Loans to related parties (note 41)	**2,668**	1,388
	Total	**23,303**	20,374

Note – Trade and other payables (extract)[2]

		2013	2012
1p77	Trade payables	**10,983**	9,495
24p18	Amounts due to related parties (note 41)	**2,202**	1,195
11p42(b)	Amounts due to customers for contract work	**997**	1,255
	Social security and other taxes	**2,002**	960
	Accrued expenses	**1,483**	828
	Total	**17,667**	13,733

Note – Construction contracts

		2013	2012
11p40(a)	The aggregate costs incurred and recognised profits (less recognised losses) to date	**69,804**	56,028
	Less: Progress billings	**(69,585)**	(56,383)
	Net balance sheet position for ongoing contracts	**219**	(355)

[1] At 31 December 2013, trade and other receivables include retentions of C232 (2012: 132) related to construction contracts in progress.
[2] At 31 December 2013, trade and other payables include customer advances of C142 (2012: C355) related to construction contracts in progress.

(All amounts in C thousands unless otherwise stated)

3. Oil and gas exploration assets

IFRS6p24   **Note – Accounting policies**

Oil and natural gas exploration and evaluation expenditures are accounted for using the 'successful efforts' method of accounting. Costs are accumulated on a field-by-field basis. Geological and geophysical costs are expensed as incurred. Costs directly associated with an exploration well, and exploration and property leasehold acquisition costs, are capitalised until the determination of reserves is evaluated. If it is determined that commercial discovery has not been achieved, these costs are charged to expense.

Capitalisation is made within property, plant and equipment or intangible assets according to the nature of the expenditure.

Once commercial reserves are found, exploration and evaluation assets are tested for impairment and transferred to development tangible and intangible assets. No depreciation and/or amortisation is charged during the exploration and evaluation phase.

(a) Development tangible and intangible assets

Expenditure on the construction, installation or completion of infrastructure facilities such as platforms, pipelines and the drilling of commercially proven development wells, is capitalised within property, plant and equipment and intangible assets according to nature. When development is completed on a specific field, it is transferred to production or intangible assets. No depreciation or amortisation is charged during the exploration and evaluation phase.

(b) Oil and gas production assets

Oil and gas production properties are aggregated exploration and evaluation tangible assets, and development expenditures associated with the production of proved reserves.

(c) Depreciation/amortisation

Expenditure on the construction, installation or completion of infrastructure facilities such as platforms, pipelines and the drilling of commercially proven development wells, is capitalised within property, plant and equipment and intangible assets according to nature. When development is completed on a specific field, it is transferred to production or intangible assets. No depreciation or amortisation is charged during the exploration and evaluation phase.

Oil and gas properties intangible assets are depreciated or amortised using the unit-of- production method. Unit-of-production rates are based on proved developed reserves, which are oil, gas and other mineral reserves estimated to be recovered from existing facilities using current operating methods. Oil and gas volumes are considered produced once they have been measured through meters at custody transfer or sales transaction points at the outlet valve on the field storage tank.

(d) Impairment – exploration and evaluation assets

Exploration and evaluation assets are tested for impairment when reclassified to development tangible or intangible assets, or whenever facts and circumstances

(All amounts in C thousands unless otherwise stated)

indicate impairment. An impairment loss is recognised for the amount by which the exploration and evaluation assets' carrying amount exceeds their recoverable amount. The recoverable amount is the higher of the exploration and evaluation assets' fair value less costs to sell and their value in use.

(e) Impairment – proved oil and gas production properties and intangible assets

Proven oil and gas properties and intangible assets are reviewed for impairment whenever events or changes in circumstances indicate that the carrying amount may not be recoverable. An impairment loss is recognised for the amount by which the asset's carrying amount exceeds its recoverable amount. The recoverable amount is the higher of an asset's fair value less costs to sell and value in use. For the purposes of assessing impairment, assets are grouped at the lowest levels for which there are separately identifiable cash flows.

Note – Property, plant and equipment[1]

	Capitalised exploration and evaluation expenditure	Capitalised development expenditure	Production assets	Other businesses and corporate assets	Total
At 1 January 2013					
Cost	218	12,450	58,720	3,951	75,339
Accumulated amortisation and impairment	(33)	–	(5,100)	(77)	(5,210)
Net book amount	185	12,450	53,620	3,874	70,129
Year ended 31 December 2013					
Opening net book amount	185	12,450	53,620	3,874	70,129
Exchange differences	17	346	1,182	325	1,870
Acquisitions	–	386	125	4	515
Additions	45	1,526	5,530	95	7,196
Transfers	(9)	(958)	1,712	–	745
Disposals	(12)	(1,687)	–	–	(1,699)
Depreciation charge	–	–	(725)	(42)	(767)
Impairment charge	(7)	(36)	(250)	(3)	(296)
Closing net book amount	**219**	**12,027**	**61,194**	**4,253**	**(1,063)**
At 31 December 2013					
Cost	264	12,027	67,019	4,330	83,640
Accumulated amortisation and impairment	(45)	–	(5,825)	(77)	(5,947)
Net book amount	**219**	**12,027**	**61,194**	**4,253**	**77,693**

[1] For the purpose of this illustrative appendix, comparatives for the year ended 31 December 2012 are not disclosed, although they are required by IAS 1.

(All amounts in C thousands unless otherwise stated)

Note – Intangible assets[1]

	Capitalised exploration and evaluation expenditure	Capitalised development expenditure	Production assets	Goodwill	Other	Total
At 1 January 2013						
Cost	5,192	750	3,412	9,475	545	19,374
Accumulated amortisation and impairment	(924)	–	(852)	(75)	(19)	(1,870)
Net book amount	4,268	750	2,560	9,400	526	17,504
Year ended 31 December 2013						
Opening net book amount	4,268	750	2,560	9,400	526	17,504
Exchange differences	152	8	195	423	28	806
Acquisitions	26	32	5	–	5	68
Additions	381	8	15	–	86	490
Transfers to production	(548)	(302)	105	–	–	(745)
Disposals	–	(28)	(15)	–	–	(43)
Amortisation charge	–	–	(98)	–	(42)	(140)
Impairment charge	(45)	–	–	(175)	(5)	(225)
Closing net book amount	**4,234**	**468**	**2,767**	**9,648**	**598**	**17,715**
At 31 December 2013						
Cost	5,203	468	3,717	9,898	659	19,945
Accumulated amortisation and impairment	(969)	–	(950)	(250)	(61)	(2,230)
Net book amount	**4,234**	**468**	**2,767**	**9,648**	**598**	**17,715**

Assets and liabilities related to the exploration and evaluation of mineral resources other than those presented above are as follows:

	2013	2012
Receivables from joint venture partners	**25**	22
Payable to subcontractors and operators	**32**	34

Exploration and evaluation activities have led to total expenses of C5,900 (2012: C5,700), of which C5,200 (2012: C4,300) are impairment charges to write off costs of unsuccessful exploration activities.

In 2013, the disposal of a 16.67% interest in an offshore exploration stage 'Field X' resulted in post-tax profits on sale of C3000 (2012: nil).

Cash payments of C41,500 (2012: C39,500) have been incurred related to exploration and evaluation activities. The cash proceeds due to the disposal of the interest in Field X were C8,000 (2012: nil).

[1] For the purpose of this illustrative appendix, comparatives for the year ended 31 December 2012 are not disclosed, although they are required by IAS 1.

(All amounts in C thousands unless otherwise stated)

4. Leases: Accounting by lessor

17p4   A lease is an agreement whereby the lessor conveys to the lessee in return for a payment, or series of payments, the right to use an asset for an agreed period of time.

Note – Accounting policies

1p119   When assets are leased out under a finance lease, the present value of the lease payments is recognised as a receivable. The difference between the gross receivable and the present value of the receivable is recognised as unearned finance income.

Commentary

Additional disclosure is required of the following for a lease:
(a)   reconciliation between the gross investment in the lease and the present value of the minimum lease payments receivable at the end of the reposting period. An entity discloses the gross investment in the lease and the present value of the minimum lease payments receivable at the end of the reporting periods:
   (i)   not later than one year;
   (ii)   later than one year and not later than five years; and
   (iii) later than five years;
(b)   unearned finance income;
(c)   the unguaranteed residual values accruing to the benefit of the lessor;
(d)   the accumulated allowance for uncollectible minimum lease payments receivable;
(e)   contingent rents recognised as income in the period; and
(f)   a general description of the lessor's material leasing arrangements.

The method for allocating gross earnings to accounting periods is referred to a as the 'actuarial method'. The actuarial method allocates rentals between finance income and repayment of capital in each accounting period in such a way that finance income will emerge as a constant rate of return on the lessor's net investment in the lease.

17p49   When assets are leased out under an operating lease, the asset is included in the balance sheet based on the nature of the asset.

17p50   Lease income on operating leases is recognised over the term of the lease on a straight-line basis.

(All amounts in C thousands unless otherwise stated)

Note – Property, plant and equipment

The category of vehicles and equipment includes vehicles leased by the group to third parties under operating leases with the following carrying amounts:

	2013	2012
Cost	70,234	83,824
Accumulated depreciation at 1 January	(14,818)	(9,800)
Depreciation charge for the year	(5,058)	(3,700)
Net book amount	50,358	70,324

17p57

Note – Trade and other receivables

	2013	2012
Non-current receivables		
Finance leases – gross receivables	1,810	630
Unearned finance income	(222)	(98)
	1,588	532
Current receivables		
Finance leases – gross receivables	1,336	316
Unearned finance income	(140)	(38)
	1,196	278
Gross receivables from finance leases:		
– No later than 1 year	1,336	316
– Later than 1 year and no later than 5 years	1,810	630
– Later than 5 years	–	–
	3,146	946
Unearned future finance income on finance leases	(362)	(136)
Net investment in finance leases	2,784	810

1p78(b)
17p47(a)
17p47(b)

The net investment in finance leases may be analysed as follows:

	2013	2012
No later than 1 year	1,196	278
Later than 1 year and no later than 5 years	1,588	532
Later than 5 years	–	–
	2,784	810

1p78(b)
17p47(a)

Note – Operating leases

Operating leases rental receivables – group company as lessor

17p56(a)

The future minimum lease payments receivable under non-cancellable operating leases are as follows:

	2013	2012
No later than 1 year	12,920	12,920
Later than 1 year and no later than 5 years	41,800	41,800
Later than 5 years	840	10,840
	55,560	65,560

(All amounts in C thousands unless otherwise stated)

17p56(b) Contingent-based rents recognised in the income statement were C235 (2012: C40).

17p56(c) The company leases vehicles under various agreements which terminate between 2013 and 2017. The agreements do not include an extension option.

5. Government grants

Note – Accounting policies

Government grants

20p39(a), p12 Grants from the government are recognised at their fair value where there is a reasonable assurance that the grant will be received and the group will comply with all attached conditions.

Government grants relating to costs are deferred and recognised in the income statement over the period necessary to match them with the costs that they are intended to compensate.

Government grants relating to property, plant and equipment are included in non-current liabilities as deferred government grants and are credited to the income statement on a straight- line basis over the expected lives of the related assets.

Note – Other (losses)/gains

20p39(b-c) The group obtained and recognised as income a government grant of C100 (2012: nil) to compensate for losses caused by flooding incurred in the previous year. The group is obliged not to reduce its average number of employees over the next three years under the terms of this government grant.

The group benefits from government assistance for promoting in international markets products made in the UK; such assistance includes marketing research and similar services provided by various UK government agencies free of charge.

6. Revenue recognition: multiple arrangements

Note – Accounting policies

The group offers certain arrangements whereby a customer can purchase a personal computer together with a two-year servicing agreement. Where such multiple-element arrangements exist, the amount of revenue allocated to each element is based upon the relative fair values of the various elements. The fair values of each element are determined based on the current market price of each of the elements when sold separately. The revenue relating to the computer is recognised when risks and rewards of the computer are transferred to the customer which occurs on delivery. Revenue relating to the service element is recognised on a straight-line basis over the service period.

(All amounts in C thousands unless otherwise stated)

7. Customer loyalty programmes

Note – Accounting policy

The Group operates a loyalty programme where customers accumulate points for purchases made which entitle them to discounts on future purchases. The reward points are recognised as a separately identifiable component of the initial sale transaction, by allocating the fair value of the consideration received between the award points and the other components of the sale such that the reward points are initially recognised as deferred income at their fair value. Revenue from the reward points is recognised when the points are redeemed. Breakage is recognised as reward points are redeemed based upon expected redemption rates. Reward points expire 12 months after the initial sale.

Note – Current liabilities – Other liabilities

	Group	
	2013	2012
Deferred revenue: customer loyalty programme	**395**	370

8. Put option arrangement

The potential cash payments related to put options issued by the group over the equity of subsidiary companies are accounted for as financial liabilities when such options may only be settled other than by exchange of a fixed amount of cash or another financial asset for a fixed number of shares in the subsidiary. The amount that may become payable under the option on exercise is initially recognised at fair value within borrowings with a corresponding charge directly to equity. The charge to equity is recognised separately as written put options over non-controlling interests, adjacent to non-controlling interests in the net assets of consolidated subsidiaries.

The group recognises the cost of writing such put options, determined as the excess of the fair value of the option over any consideration received, as a financing cost. Such options are subsequently measured at amortised cost, using the effective interest rate method, in order to accrete the liability up to the amount payable under the option at the date at which it first becomes exercisable. The charge arising is recorded as a financing cost. In the event that the option expires unexercised, the liability is derecognised with a corresponding adjustment to equity.

9. Foreign currency translations – disposal of foreign operation and partial disposal

21p48, 48A-C On the disposal of a foreign operation (that is, a disposal of the group's entire interest in a foreign operation, or a disposal involving loss of control over a subsidiary that includes a foreign operation, a disposal involving loss of joint control over a jointly controlled entity that includes a foreign operation, or a disposal involving loss of significant influence over an associate that includes a foreign operation), all of the exchange differences accumulated in equity in respect of that operation attributable to the equity holders of the company are reclassified to profit or loss.

(All amounts in C thousands unless otherwise stated)

In the case of a partial disposal that does not result in the group losing control over a subsidiary that includes a foreign operation, the proportionate share of accumulated exchange differences are re-attributed to non-controlling interests and are not recognised in profit or loss. For all other partial disposals (that is, reductions in the group's ownership interest in associates or jointly controlled entities that do not result in the group losing significant influence or joint control) the proportionate share of the accumulated exchange difference is reclassified to profit or loss.

10. Share-based payments – modification and cancellation

IFRS2p27

If the terms of an equity-settled award are modified, at a minimum an expense is recognised as if the terms had not been modified. An additional expense is recognised for any modification that increases the total fair value of the share-based payment arrangement, or is otherwise beneficial to the employee, as measured at the date of modification.

IFRS2
p28(a),(c)

If an equity-settled award is cancelled, it is treated as if it had vested on the date of cancellation, and any expense not yet recognised for the award is recognised immediately. However, if a new award is substituted for the cancelled award, and designated as a replacement award on the date that it is granted, the cancelled and new award are treated as if they were a modification of the original award, as described in the previous paragraph.

If an equity award is cancelled by forfeiture, when the vesting conditions (other than market conditions) have not been met, any expense not yet recognised for that award, as at the date of forfeiture, is treated as if it had never been recognised. At the same time, any expense previously recognised on such cancelled equity awards are reversed from the accounts effective as at the date of forfeiture.

The dilutive effect, if any, of outstanding options is reflected as additional share dilution in the computation of earnings per share.

(All amounts in C thousands unless otherwise stated)

Appendix IV – New standards and amendments

This appendix details (a) new standards and amendments effective for the first time for periods beginning on or after 1 January 2013 and (b) forthcoming requirements – that is, new standards and amendments issued and effective after 1 January 2013.

New standards and amendments

Below is a list of standards/interpretations that have been issued and are effective for periods beginning on or after 1 January 2013.

Topic	Key requirements	Effective date
Amendment to IAS 1, 'Financial statement presentation', regarding other comprehensive income	The main change resulting from these amendments is a requirement for entities to group items presented in 'other comprehensive income' (OCI) on the basis of whether they are potentially reclassifiable to profit or loss subsequently (reclassification adjustments). The amendments do not address which items are presented in OCI.	1 July 2012
Amendment to IAS 19, 'Employee benefits'	These amendments eliminate the corridor approach and calculate finance costs on a net funding basis.	1 January 2013
Amendment to IFRS 1, 'First time adoption', on government loans	This amendment addresses how a first-time adopter would account for a government loan with a below-market rate of interest when transitioning to IFRS. It also adds an exception to the retrospective application of IFRS, which provides the same relief to first-time adopters granted to existing preparers of IFRS financial statements when the requirement was incorporated into IAS 20 in 2008.	1 January 2013
Amendment to IFRS 7, 'Financial instruments: Disclosures', on asset and liability offsetting	This amendment includes new disclosures to facilitate comparison between those entities that prepare IFRS financial statements to those that prepare financial statements in accordance with US GAAP.	1 January 2013
Amendment to IFRSs 10, 11 and 12 on transition guidance	These amendments provide additional transition relief to IFRSs 10, 11 and 12, limiting the requirement to provide adjusted comparative information to only the preceding comparative period. For disclosures related to unconsolidated structured entities, the amendments will remove the requirement to present comparative information for periods before IFRS 12 is first applied.	1 January 2013
Annual improvements 2011	These annual improvements, address six issues in the 2009-2011 reporting cycle. It includes changes to: • IFRS 1, 'First time adoption' • IAS 1, 'Financial statement presentation' • IAS 16, 'Property plant and equipment' • IAS 32, 'Financial instruments; Presentation' • IAS 34, 'Interim financial reporting'	1 January 2013

(All amounts in C thousands unless otherwise stated)

Topic	Key requirements	Effective date
IFRS 10, 'Consolidated financial statements'	The objective of IFRS 10 is to establish principles for the presentation and preparation of consolidated financial statements when an entity controls one or more other entity (an entity that controls one or more other entities) to present consolidated financial statements. It defines the principle of control, and establishes controls as the basis for consolidation. It sets out how to apply the principle of control to identify whether an investor controls an investee and therefore must consolidate the investee. It also sets out the accounting requirements for the preparation of consolidated financial statements.	1 January 2013
IFRS 11, 'Joint arrangements'	IFRS 11 is a more realistic reflection of joint arrangements by focusing on the rights and obligations of the arrangement rather than its legal form. There are two types of joint arrangement: joint operations and joint ventures. Joint operations arise where a joint operator has rights to the assets and obligations relating to the arrangement and therefore accounts for its interest in assets, liabilities, revenue and expenses. Joint ventures arise where the joint operator has rights to the net assets of the arrangement and therefore equity accounts for its interest. Proportional consolidation of joint ventures is no longer allowed.	1 January 2013
IFRS 12, 'Disclosures of interests in other entities'	IFRS 12 includes the disclosure requirements for all forms of interests in other entities, including joint arrangements, associates, special purpose vehicles and other off balance sheet vehicles.	1 January 2013
IFRS 13, 'Fair value measurement'	IFRS 13 aims to improve consistency and reduce complexity by providing a precise definition of fair value and a single source of fair value measurement and disclosure requirements for use across IFRSs. The requirements, which are largely aligned between IFRS and US GAAP, do not extend the use of fair value accounting but provide guidance on how it should be applied where its use is already required or permitted by other standards within IFRSs or US GAAP.	1 January 2013
IAS 27 (revised 2011), 'Separate financial statements'	IAS 27 (revised 2011) includes the provisions on separate financial statements that are left after the control provisions of IAS 27 have been included in the new IFRS 10.	1 January 2013
IAS 28 (revised 2011), 'Associates and joint ventures'	IAS 28 (revised 2011) includes the requirements for joint ventures, as well as associates, to be equity accounted following the issue of IFRS 11.	1 January 2013
IFRIC 20, 'Stripping costs in the production phase of a surface mine'	This interpretation sets out the accounting for overburden waste removal (stripping) costs in the production phase of a mine. The interpretation may require mining entities reporting under IFRS to write off existing stripping assets to opening retained earnings if the assets cannot be attributed to an identifiable component of an ore body.	1 January 2013

(All amounts in C thousands unless otherwise stated)

Forthcoming requirements

Below is a list of standards/interpretations that have been issued and are effective for periods after 1 January 2013.

Topic	Key requirements	Effective date
Amendment to IAS 32, 'Financial instruments: Presentation', on asset and liability offsetting	These amendments are to the application guidance in IAS 32, 'Financial instruments: Presentation', and clarify some of the requirements for offsetting financial assets and financial liabilities on the balance sheet.	1 January 2014
Amendments to IFRS 10, 12 and IAS 27 on consolidation for investment entities	These amendments mean that many funds and similar entities will be exempt from consolidating most of their subsidiaries. Instead, they will measure them at fair value through profit or loss. The amendments give an exception to entities that meet an 'investment entity' definition and which display particular characteristics. Changes have also been made IFRS 12 to introduce disclosures that an investment entity needs to make.	1 January 2014
Amendment to IAS 36, 'Impairment of assets' on recoverable amount disclosures	This amendment addresses the disclosure of information about the recoverable amount of impaired assets if that amount is based on fair value less costs of disposal.	1 January 2014
Financial Instruments: Recognition and Measurement Amendment to IAS 39 'Novation of derivatives'	This amendment provides relief from discontinuing hedge accounting when novation ot a hedging instrument to a central counter party meets specified criteria.	1 January 2014
IFRIC 21, 'Levies'	This is an interpretation of IAS 37, 'Provisions, contingent liabilities and contingent assets'. IAS 37 sets out criteria for the recognition of a liability, one of which is the requirement for the entity to have a present obligation as a result of a past event (known as an obligating event). The interpretation clarifies that the obligating event that gives rise to a liability to pay a levy is the activity described in the relevant legislation that triggers the payment of the levy.	1 January 2014
IFRS 9, 'Financial instruments'	IFRS 9 is the first standard issued as part of a wider project to replace IAS 39. IFRS 9 retains but simplifies the mixed measurement model and establishes two primary measurement categories for financial assets: amortised cost and fair value. The basis of classification depends on the entity's business model and the contractual cash flow characteristics of the financial asset. The guidance in IAS 39 on impairment of financial assets and hedge accounting continues to apply.	See Appendix V

(All amounts in C thousands unless otherwise stated)

Appendix V – IFRS 9, 'Financial instruments'

PwC commentary – IFRS 9

IFRS9p7.2.14 As part of the Limited Amendments to IFRS 9 project, the IASB tentatively decided at the July 2013 board meeting to defer the mandatory effective date of IFRS 9. The IASB agreed that the mandatory effective date should no longer be annual periods beginning on or after 1 January 2015 but rather be left open pending the finalisation of the impairment and classification and measurement requirements. As a result of these decisions and the changes being proposed to IFRS 9, the transitional guidance will change.

IFRS 9 is currently still available for early application. If the entity adopts IFRS 9 (2010) for annual periods on or after 1 January 2013, it provides the disclosures required by IFRS 7 as amended in December 2011 and does not need to restate prior periods.

For an entity considering adopting IFRS 9, an example of the disclosures relating to the implementation of IFRS 9 are included as Appendix VI to PwC's "Illustrative IFRS consolidated financial statements for 2012 year ends".

Note that the IFRS 9 appendix VI disclosures in the "Illustrative IFRS consolidated financial statements for 2012 year ends" have not been updated for changes in IFRS standards, in particular IFRSs 10, 11, 12 and 13 and the amendments to IAS 1 and IAS 19.